KÖNIGS ERLÄUTERUNGEN SPEZIAL

W0075200

Textanalyse und Interpretation zu

Sindiwe Magona

MOTHER TO MOTHER

Patrick Charles

Analyse | Interpretation in englischer Sprache

Zitierte Ausgabe:
Magona, Sindiwe: *Mother to Mother.* Stuttgart: Ernst Klett Sprachen, 2016.

Über den Autor dieser Erläuterung:
Patrick Charles wurde 1973 in Bournemouth, Südengland, geboren und studierte englische Literatur an der Universität von Newcastle. 1993 zog er nach Berlin, wo er eine Ausbildung zum Buchhändler machte und zehn Jahre lang als Buchhändler arbeitete. Seit 2004 ist er als freiberuflicher Autor von Schulbüchern und Lernhilfen und als Übersetzer im Kulturbereich tätig. Er lebt mit seiner Familie in Berlin.

2. Auflage 2019
ISBN: 978-3-8044-3132-4
PDF: 978-3-8044-5132-2, EPUB: 978-3-8044-4132-3
© 2017 by Bange Verlag GmbH, 96142 Hollfeld
Alle Rechte vorbehalten!
Titelabbildung: © svetazi/Fotolia
Druck und Weiterverarbeitung: Tiskárna Akcent, Vimperk

1. **AT A GLANCE –**   6
    THE MOST IMPORTANT POINTS

2. **SINDIWE MAGONA: LIFE & WORKS**   9

    2.1 **Biography** ——————————————————— 9
    2.2 **Contemporary Background** —————————— 11
        Geography ——————————————————— 11
        Apartheid in South Africa ————————————— 14
        The Xhosa ——————————————————— 21
    2.3 **Notes on Other Important Works** —————————— 28

3. **ANALYSES AND INTERPRETATIONS**   31

    3.1 **Origins and Sources** ——————————————— 31
        Guguletu ——————————————————— 31
        The murder of Amy Biehl ————————————— 32
        Police ————————————————————— 35
        The author's life and experiences ————————— 36
    3.2 **Summaries** ————————————————————— 37
        1 - Mandisa's Lament (p. 1) ——————————— 37
        2 - Mowbray – Wednesday 25 August 1993 (p. 5) —— 38
        3 - 5.15 pm – Wednesday 25 August 1993 (p. 20) —— 39
        4 - 7.30 pm (p. 40) ——————————————— 40
        5 (p. 48) —————————————————————— 40
        6 - 4 am – Thursday 28 August 1993 (p. 79) ————— 44
        7 (p. 88) —————————————————————— 44
        8 (p. 115) ————————————————————— 47

9 - 6 am Thursday 26 August (p. 164) _____ 50
10 (p. 173) _____ 51
11 (p. 198) _____ 53
12 (p. 203) _____ 54
3.3 Structure _____ 55
The narrative perspective – mother to mother _____ 56
Layers of memories _____ 57
Thoughts and memories _____ 59
3.4 Characters _____ 62
Mandisa _____ 63
Mxolisi _____ 66
Lunga _____ 71
Siziwe _____ 71
China _____ 72
Lungile _____ 73
Dwadwa _____ 74
Mandisa's extended family _____ 74
China's family _____ 77
Friends and neighbours _____ 77
The other mother _____ 79
The dead white girl _____ 79
Other secondary characters _____ 80
Constellations _____ 81
3.5 Themes _____ 84
IDENTITY & INEQUALITY _____ 84
VIOLENCE, HATRED & DEHUMANISATION _____ 92
COMMUNITY, FAMILY, TRADITION & HISTORY ____ 100
GUILT, HOPE, DESPAIR & COPING WITH GRIEF ____ 108
THE ORGANISING THEME _____ 113

3.6 Style and Language ———————————— 114

A subjective and emotional narrative voice ———— 114

Use of Xhosa ———————————————— 116

Archaic and unusual diction ————————— 117

3.7 Approaches to Interpretation —————— 119

4. CRITICAL RECEPTION   126

5. MATERIALS   128

A brief overview of the history of South Africa ———— 128

Amy Biehl ———————————————— 130

Some useful terms ————————————— 132

6. SAMPLE EXAM QUESTIONS AND ANSWERS   135

SOURCES & REFERENCES   141

INDEX   144

1. AT A GLANCE –
THE MOST IMPORTANT POINTS

This study guide to Sindiwe Magona's novel *Mother to Mother* is designed to provide an easy-to-use overview of the structure, context, themes and characters of the novel. Here is a quick rundown of the most important points.

Part 2 takes a brief look at **Sindiwe Magona and her career**.

⇨ p. 9
→ Magona was **born in 1943** in the village of Gungululu in South Africa. She has written a multi-volume autobiography, novels, short stories, poetry and biographies.

⇨ p. 11
→ *Mother to Mother* is a semi-autobiographical fictionalised account of the **murder of a white american girl** (Amy Biehl) and describes the era and aftermath of apartheid in South Africa.

Part 3 offers analyses and interpretations of the novel.

Mother to Mother – Origins and sources:

⇨ p. 31
The novel is set in places where Magona lived and during a time when she was also living there. It draws heavily on her own life and experience, and looks at the lives of Xhosa people in the townships of South Africa.

Summaries:

⇨ p. 37
The narrator is a mother of three called Mandisa. Her eldest son Mxolisi has been involved with a group of student protesters in the township of Guguletu, near Cape Town. In August 1993 he gets caught up in a mob which assaults and kills a white girl in a car.

The novel is in the form of Mandisa's address directly to the dead girl's mother. She tells the story of her life and how she had

Mxolisi when she was just 15. Her story covers her childhood in the slums of Blouvlei, the government-ordered forced resettlement of the people from there to the township of Guguletu near Cape Town, where families and communities were torn apart, and her struggles to raise her children. Throughout her life she and her children have been witness to and victims of racist oppression and brutality from the police. She moves back and forth in time as she tells her story, explaining how things happened the way they did.

Structure:

The novel is about the origins of events and their consequences, so it moves back and forth in time to illustrate how Mxolisi came to be the troubled, disobedient and violent young man he is in 1993. It also includes descriptions of specific episodes in South African history, as well as stories from Xhosa history and the origins of the hatred and racism in the country.

⇨ p. 55

Characters:

Mandisa and her son Mxolisi are central to everything that happens and everything the novel is about.

Mandisa
⇨ p. 63
→ the narrator, mother of three children
→ she became accidentally pregnant when she was 14

Mxolisi
⇨ p. 66
→ Mandisa's eldest son, who kills the white girl

Lunga and Siziwe
⇨ p. 71
→ Mandisa's second son and her daughter

⇨ p. 72   **China, Lungile & Dwadwa**
→ Mandisa's three husbands and the fathers of her children

⇨ p. 74   **Mandisa's extended family** (Mama, Tata, Khaya, et al.)

⇨ p. 77   **Other characters** like China's family, Mandisa's friends and neighbours or the white girl and her mother

Themes:

⇨ p. 84   The themes we will look at in this study guide are issues of identity and inequality: violence and oppression; communities, families and traditions; and grief, guilt, hope and despair. There is a larger theme behind all of these which organises the structure of the narrative, and that is an investigation of the past.

Style and language:

⇨ p. 114   The style of the novel moves between a clear and direct address (from "me" to "you") and a richer, poetic style. The language is an interesting combination of unusual English diction and structures and a mixture of the various languages people of Mandisa's status would speak – English, Afrikaans and Xhosa.

Interpretations:

⇨ p. 119   *Mother to Mother* can be interpreted and read as both an informative, semi-autobiographical fictionalised account of the killing of Amy Biehl and as a look at bigger historical issues and symbolism.

2. SINDIWE MAGONA: LIFE & WORKS

2.1 Biography

YEAR	PLACE	EVENT	AGE
1943	Gungululu (village in what is now called the Eastern Cape, formerly Transkei), South Africa	27 August: Sindiwe Magona is born, eldest of eight children	
1962	Gugulethu	She works for years as a junior school teacher.	19
1966	Gugulethu	Already the mother of two children, Magona is now pregnant with a third when her husband leaves the family.	23
1981	Gugulethu	Completes a graduate degree (her third academic degree) from Columbia University (USA) via post.	38
1980s–2000s	New York, USA	Magona moves with her family to New York to work at the United Nations.	Late 30s–60
1993	New York	Awarded an Honorary Degree in Humane Letters by Hartwick College in Oneonta (New York State, USA).	50
Up to 1994	New York	Works for the UN, presenting anti-apartheid radio programmes.	51
1990	Cape Town, South Africa	Publication of the first part of her autobiography *To My Children's Children*.	47
1998	Cape Town	***Mother to Mother* was published**.	55
2003	New York/Cape Town	Magona has been working for the UN's Public Information Department before retiring in 2003 and moving back to South Africa.	60

Sindiwe Magona (*1943)
© picture alliance/ Scanpix TT NEWS AGENCY

2.1 Biography

YEAR	PLACE	EVENT	AGE
2003–now	Cape Town	Writer in Residence at the University of the Western Cape in Cape Town; also works for Georgia State University (USA).	
2007	South Africa	In this year, Magona is awarded several major prizes. She is presented with the Lifetime Achievement Award for her contributions to South African Literature, as well as other prizes recognising her literary work, her social activism and her efforts to promote and celebrate Xhosa culture.	64
2012	South Africa	2012 she is joint winner with Nadine Gordimer of the Mbokodo Award in Creative Writing.[1]	69

----

1   http://www.mbokodoawards.co.za/mbokodo_awards_2012_winners.html

2.2 Contemporary Background

SUMMARY

→ *Mother to Mother* is set in the Western Cape province of South Africa and covers a period from the early 1970s up until 1993.
→ The book describes the era and aftermath of apartheid in South Africa and is the real world backdrop to the murder of Amy Biehl in August 1993.

Mother to Mother is set in the **Western Cape province** of South Africa and covers a period from **the early 1970s up until 1993**. The story is largely situated in a black township near Cape Town called **Guguletu**. Other locations include the squatters' settlement of Blouvlei, where Mandisa grew up, and her ancestral village Gungululu, where her grandmother still lives. All the African characters in the novel belong to the Xhosa people, and we see many examples of tribal customs and traditions.

The book describes the era and aftermath of apartheid in South Africa, a period of extreme **racial oppression, state neglect, police brutality and political turmoil and violence**. This is the real world backdrop to **the murder of Amy Biehl in August 1993** (see p. 32); the novel is a fictionalised account of the killing.

Apartheid system in South Africa

Geography
Guguletu
The majority of the book – and the entirety of its present-day time frame, in 1993 – is set in the township of Guguletu, which is 15 kilometres outside Cape Town, in the Western Cape province of South Africa. Today Guguletu has a population of over 98,000, and **more**

2.2 Contemporary Background

than 98% are black Africans. The primary language spoken in the township is Xhosa.

1960s: Township for black people

Guguletu (which comes from the Xhosa phrase for "our pride", igugu lethu) was founded in the 1960s as a home for the black people of the Cape Town district of Langa. During apartheid, blacks in the region were not allowed to live in Cape Town and were forced to live in one district, which became desperately overcrowded. Residents were relocated to Guguletu and other newly-founded townships, where overcrowding, **lack of education, jobs and adequate infrastructure** (electricity, running water, waste removal, etc.) greatly increased social tensions. Guguletu is infamous for its **high levels of crime**, including world-famous murders like that of Amy Biehl, and it remains a troubled and problem-ridden community even in the 21st century, with an estimated murder every two and a half days between 2005 and 2010[2].

Blouvlei

Blouvlei is the squatters' settlement where Mandisa remembers growing up, before her family was forcibly relocated to Guguletu. Blouvlei was founded by squatters – people who occupy land or buildings without permission and without paying rent. It was one of three major squatters' settlements, the others being Windermere and Epping Forest, which were founded by people coming south to find work in Cape Town during and after the Second World War. They were estimated to be home to roughly 20,000 people each. **Cape Town was a "closed city"** (blacks were not allowed to live there) and there was very little employment or hope for jobs. Poverty was widespread amongst the black population.[3]

---

2 https://mg.co.za/article/2010-11-16-over-700-murders-in-gugulethu-since-2005
3 http://www.capetown.at/heritage/history/1910_dev_immig_art.htm

2.2 Contemporary Background

Successive governments made efforts to redirect some of the migrants to a "reception depot" in Langa, which itself became terribly overcrowded. After the war, some settlers were allowed by the local council to buy the land they had occupied, but the national government took control of everything related to housing across the country and **began to relocate black Africans** as a part of the efforts to enforce segregation.

There were **groups of civil rights activists in Blouvlei** who worked to resist the forced relocations as part of their struggles against the apartheid system. As Mandisa explains in the novel, however, these efforts were futile, because the government used police and the military to literally destroy the settlements, forcing the inhabitants cross-country to the newly-founded segregated townships like Guguletu.

Resettlement enforced by police and military

Gungululu

Mandisa is sent away from Guguletu to live with her grandmother in the ancestral village where her mother was born. This is **a very different world** from the one she has known so far in her fourteen years: It is a traditional tribal village where old customs are still in effect and there are none of the amenities of even the township slums. Mandisa is lovesick for China and does not adapt easily to the village.

Gungululu is the name of a district as well as of the village, and is situated in the Eastern Cape region – Mandisa describes it as comprising "some twenty or so villages" (p. 101). This is also where the author Sindiwe Magona was born (see Chapter 2.1). At the time covered in the novel, the village and the region were a **part of the Transkei**, which existed as a state (although unrecognised by the South African government) from 1976 to 1994.

2.2 Contemporary Background

Lovesick Mandisa

The village is presented in an ambiguous way in the novel (pp. 88–114). Mandisa's reaction is predictably and even understandably negative – she is a teenager from a bustling township, torn away from her boyfriend and stuck in a **backwards village in the middle of nowhere**. She complains that the village is "remote", but worse, she is "separated from China" (p. 108). But there is a simplicity and a calm in the village which she appreciates, and she admits that the place isn't bad and that the school is good (p. 108). As is the case with the traditions and customs that have so much influence over her life, Mandisa is frustrated and restrained by rural life, yet appreciates its rooted, solid essence.

Apartheid in South Africa

Apartheid (meaning literally "separateness") was a system of **racial segregation** in South Africa. It existed as a state-ordered policy determining South African society from 1948 until 1991.[4]

Segregation

> **Segregation** is the act or policy of separating people of different races, religions or genders, and treating them differently. Many cultures across the world and throughout history, from 8th century China to 13th century Europe and the USA in the 20th century, have practiced segregation in order to separate people of different races in daily life. Even following the end of apartheid in South Africa, segregation by race, religion and gender still exists in various countries all around the world.

---

4   http://www.bpb.de/politik/hintergrund-aktuell/219628/apartheid-gesetze

2.2 Contemporary Background

The apartheid system was based on a very simple ideology – **white supremacy**. The fundamental idea was that white-skinned people are in every way superior to darker-skinned people, and that **blacks must be repressed and segregated** in order to benefit the white ruling class. This repression and segregation was the form that apartheid took and the guiding principle for how society was structured. The white rulers were predominantly Afrikaners, who were descended from the Dutch colonists of the 17th and 18th centuries. They maintained a firm grip on politics, the economy and land ownership and had, since the 17th century, enforced increasingly strict and regulated racial divisions and separations. The development of apartheid – from isolated, casual racist oppression within regions and communities to outright national policy – was gradual, taking over two centuries, and **it then lasted in its most strict and brutal form for a little less than fifty years**.

White ruling class

A very brief history of apartheid

Pre-20th century racial oppression and discrimination was more freewheeling and casual: there was a slave era, the increasing theft of land and resources from native peoples by European (mostly Dutch) settlers, and with the coming of the British there was a rise in industrialisation and a great expansion of mining projects (South Africa is home to some of the most profitable diamond mines on the planet, with roughly 49% of all diamonds still being mined in Central and South Africa). Black people were pushed off their land when the white settlers wanted to use it themselves; they were **forbidden from living in certain places and doing certain work;** they were not allowed to vote or enter white churches; and criminal acts against blacks were barely noticed and rarely dealt with seriously by white authorities. The Dutch settlers had already introduced a **hierarchy of race**, with whites at the top, In-

Black Miners

Not allowed to vote

2.2 Contemporary Background

dians and Asians somewhere in the middle, and blacks at the very bottom.

By the mid-20th century, however, the central government began to institute stricter and more precise legislation to enforce the system of white supremacy.

→ **The Prohibition of Mixed Marriages Act in 1949** is considered to be the first step in the institutionalisation of white supremacy as state policy. This law, and the **Immorality Act** of the following year, made it a crime to marry or have sexual relationships across racial lines.

→ Another 1950 law, **the Population Registration Act**, defined the four legal racial groups: black, white, coloured and Indian. Your race defined where you could live, what job you could have, and who you were allowed to interact with. Identification papers included these racial designations, and citizens were not able to cross the boundaries of their assigned region without these papers.

→ In 1953 **the Reservation of Separate Amenities Act** defined racially-specific public services, such as hospitals, universities and public parks, which were not allowed to be used by members of other races.

→ Also passed in 1953, **the Bantu Education Act** segregated national education, effectively cutting black South Africans off from the better-financed and organised educational infrastructure, which was from this point on only available to whites.

→ In the 1950s the government also created the **"pass laws"**, which stopped black South Africans from being able to travel freely in the country. The pass laws in particular limited blacks' ability to enter urban areas; black South Africans were now required to provide authorisation from a white employer to be

2.2 Contemporary Background

able to enter specific towns and cities (when China vanishes, Mandisa first believes he may have been arrested for just this crime: "Maybe he had been arrested for a pass offence", p. 144).

These laws led to the forced relocations of the 1960s–1980s, dur- Tribal homelands
ing which millions of non-white Africans were removed from their homes and made to live in so-called "tribal homelands" – although these areas often had no historical validity or relevance for the tribes. These regions were also largely unsuitable for larger populations, with **very poor agricultural potential and little or no infrastructure**. Some of these so-called bantustans became independent republics. The goal of the white supremacist governments was to strip black Africans of their South African citizenship as they moved into the bantustans, thus **removing all remaining rights from the blacks** and freeing the white rulers of all remaining responsibility for the blacks.

Petty and grand apartheid – Very broadly speaking, apartheid in South Africa came in two forms. Petty apartheid is the segregation of public facilities (hospitals, public toilets, churches, public transport etc.) and social events, meaning that blacks and whites are not allowed – by law – to share these facilities or to mix with one another in "social events". Grand apartheid is concerned with housing and employment. So the relocations which play such a huge role in Mandisa's youth are an example of grand apartheid: the government telling her and her family where they are allowed to live (see p. 28, where Mandisa describes the shock of being relocated to Guguletu). Black labour was necessary to uphold South Africa's indus-

2.2   Contemporary Background

tries – particularly mining – because the blacks could be exploited with poor wages, little or no labour law protections, and inadequate security for dangerous jobs. This government control of work is also a case of grand apartheid.

UN: crime against humanity

The apartheid system was hugely controversial and widely denounced all around the world. As well as activism and resistance within South Africa, there were global movements aimed at stopping and removing the institution of white supremacy as state policy. Many countries joined in arms and **trade embargoes against South Africa**. In 1973 the United Nations officially defined the apartheid system as a crime against humanity, which would allow criminal prosecution of individuals responsible for upholding and enforcing the system. Not all member states signed the declaration: by 2008, nearly 90 states had still not signed.

Sports

Sport under apartheid – The world of sports is not relevant to *Mother to Mother*, but a brief look at the subject highlights the injustice and absurdity of white supremacist policies on a social as well as international level. Because the apartheid system forbids multiracial sports teams, it was almost impossible for teams from other countries to play any kind of sports in South Africa. No teams were permitted to compete if they contained members of different races.

The International Table Tennis Federation cut all ties to the South African table tennis organisations in protest. South Africa was banned from the 1964 Olympics, and again in 1968.

2.2 Contemporary Background

The Australian Cricketing Association refused to compete in South Africa or against South African teams as long as they selected their teams on a purely racial basis. In the Chess Olympiad of 1970, the Albanian team forfeited rather than face a team of chess players from an apartheid state. South Africa was suspended from FIFA (the international governing body for football) in 1963. The South African tennis team was banned from the 1970 Davis Cup tournament, and when they were allowed to participate in 1974 they won because the Indian team refused to travel to South Africa to compete in the final.

Following the end of apartheid in 1991, the various boycotts against South African athletes and teams also quickly ended.

By the 1980s increasing number of Western companies and organisations were withdrawing from South Africa in response to louder and louder calls for **boycotts and embargoes**, taking their money with them, and this, combined with structural flaws in the South African economy, was having a devastating effect on the country. These economic pressures combined with increasingly potent and at times violent resistance within the country, as militant and activist groups grew bolder and angrier. Under increased pressure from within and from the rest of the world, the South African government began to release anti-apartheid political prisoners, which further electrified and revitalised anti-apartheid activism within the country as these political prisoners – or, in the phrase made famous by Amnesty International, "prisoners of conscience" – were welcomed back as heroes and martyrs by the anti-apartheid movement.

Economic and social pressure

2.2 Contemporary Background

Attempts made by the central government to reform apartheid – such as giving "coloureds" and "Indians" voting rights in 1983 – were widely seen as inadequate responses to the problem. The government under **P. W. Botha** (1916–2006, leader of South Africa from 1978 to 1989) claimed it was about to make reforms to the apartheid laws which never came true.

Release of Nelson Mandela in 1990

By the **end of the 1980s** the South African economy was in terrible shape, and when Botha suffered a stroke and resigned as leader, **F. W. de Klerk** became the leader of the state, and moved quickly to begin dismantling the discriminatory legislation underpinning apartheid. The changes he initiated included lifting the bans on anti-apartheid groups and organisations like Nelson Mandela's ANC (African National Congress). De Klerk also ordered **the release from prison of Mandela after 27 years**, restored the freedom of the press and suspended the death penalty. De Klerk was the country's president in 1993, when the contemporary events surrounding the murder of the white girl are described in the novel.

The end of apartheid

The end of apartheid was finalised in a series of negotiations in the years 1990 and 1991, ending in the general elections of 1994 (a year following the events described in *Mother to Mother*), the first time in the country's history that **all South Africans were allowed to vote**. The process was violent, with both "black on black" violence erupting all over the country as well as white supremacist attacks on anti-apartheid activists and even assassinations of anti-apartheid leaders. The negotiations were repeatedly interrupted by protests from groups and organisations representing the far-right white racist minority. The violence continued right up until the day of the general election, with car bombs exploding and people being killed. On April 27, 1994, the apartheid state officially ceased to exist, and South Africa raised its new flag and sang the new official national anthem, "God Bless Africa".

2.2   Contemporary Background

The novel is very much about the apartheid era – about the forces (racism and colonialism) which made it possible, the terrible consequences it had for society as a whole, and for tribes, families and individuals. Sindiwe Magona is a generation older than her main character, Mandisa, and Mandisa's experiences are based on Magona's own life, specifically the places she was forced to live and the pressures on her as a black woman and a young mother. Magona was born in 1943 and witnessed the apartheid era in its entirety; as an adult she campaigned ceaselessly from the UN in New York for an end to apartheid.

Sindiwe Magona's
Mother to Mother

The Xhosa

Mandisa and her family (and the other African characters we see in the novel) are all Xhosa. There are 8 million Xhosa people living in South Africa (roughly 18% of the population, according to the 2011 census). They are an ethnic sub-group of the Bantu peoples, which is the umbrella term for the hundreds of ethnic groups in Africa who speak variants of the Bantu languages. The language spoken by the Xhosa is called isiXhosa, and it is the second most commonly spoken language in South Africa (after Zulu).

During apartheid, the Xhosa were denied South African citizenship, and were instead allowed to live in self-governed so-called "homelands", called Transkei and Ciskei.

The cattle killing movement: "The hatred has but multiplied."

The cattle killing movement of 1854–1858 was a near-catastrophic act of self-destruction committed by the Xhosa, based on a prophecy by a young girl. Cattle introduced by the white settlers had spread new diseases to the native cattle, many of which died. The loss of cattle – which were for the Xhosa an important status symbol as well as being a source of food and leather (see pp. 176–177) – was

Many Xhosa died

2.2   Contemporary Background

a serious problem. The girl, Nongqawuse, told her father that she had encountered spirits out in the fields, and that they had told her that the Xhosa should kill all of their cattle. The spirits of all the dead Xhosa would then return to drive out the white settlers, and bring back all the cattle with them (p. 180).

Her prophecy made its way to the chief of the Xhosa, who ordered the tribe **to kill all their cattle and destroy all their grain supplies**. Some Xhosa allegedly believed the prophecy to be genuine, and some simply followed orders. Whatever their reasons may have been, the results were disastrous. Famine struck, the Xhosa had no food, the prophesied return of the ancestors never happened and the dead cattle never reappeared. Instead, the white European settlers were forbidden by their governor Sir George Grey from helping the starving, helpless Xhosa unless the tribespeople signed labour contracts with the white landowners. The Xhosa were then bound to work in the mines, labouring for the white colonists.

Mandisa and her grandfather Tatomkhulu

This is told to Mandisa by her grandfather Tatomkhulu (see Chapter 10, pp. 175–183). A true story and an important episode in **Xhosa history**, the story has additional significance to the novel. Mandisa has been taught that the Xhosa followed the prophecy because they were "superstitious and ignorant" (p. 175). But her grandfather teaches her that it was an act of desperation, fed by their hatred of the white settlers who had stolen absolutely everything from the native peoples of the country they had colonised – a colossal, catastrophic act of self-harm. Mandisa comes to believe that the story reveals something honourable rather than merely being a display of disastrous ignorance. Her grandfather positions it in a sequence of protests and uprisings against the white settlers through the colonial history of South Africa, pointing out efforts by the black inhabitants of the country to reclaim their land which had been stolen from them, and to resist the "button without a hole" – meaning coins, because

2.2 Contemporary Background

money was unknown to pre-colonial South Africa – because of the damaging effect money would have on a purely agrarian culture.

The symbolism of this history of honourable but doomed protests and violent, apocalyptic uprisings against the hated white oppressors is of great relevance to the tragic story of the killing of the white girl in Guguletu – the story at the heart of *Mother to Mother*. The same hatred of colonists who had stolen everything can be seen in both the cattle killing movement of 1857 and the "one settler, one bullet!" war cry of the furious **anti-apartheid protests** of the 1980s and 1990s, and the mob who killed Amy Biehl.

White oppressors: "one settler, one bullet!"

Rites of passage and traditions:
Marriage, parenthood and gender

We see different examples of traditional customs and rites of passage in the novel, and learn about the traditions which organise marriage, the business of parenthood and the roles and interaction of men and women. These traditions are seen with **a degree of ambivalence**: While Mandisa is frustrated by the unfairness of the limits imposed on her as a woman and a young mother, and is equally annoyed by the dominance allowed to males within the culture, she also sees how a lack of traditions and respect for customs and cultural roles can damage and break a society.

Ambivalence of traditions

We will look at the role played by traditional initiation rites and customs in the chapter on themes in the novel (see p. 100). These include:

→ Marriage arrangements and ceremonies
→ Circumcision and coming of age rites for young men
→ Naming customs
→ The patriarchal structure of tribal society
→ Tribal legends and myths
→ Faith healers (Sangomas)

2.2 Contemporary Background

Education and politics

"Boycotts, strikes and indifference have plagued the schools in the last two decades. Our children have paid the price." (Mandisa, p. 72)

Poster from 1985 protesting and demanding reform of the education system.[5]

The combination of inadequate education, social neglect and bad politics (at once irresponsible, oppressive politics proved to be explosive in the immediate aftermath of the apartheid regime. **The protests and explosions of violence** which Sindiwe Magona talks about in *Mother to Mother* were shocking to many – to locals and neighbours as well as outsiders and foreign observers.

The apartheid system influenced education as well as every other aspect of life in South Africa. From the early 1980s, black schools were legally required to conduct the majority of their lessons in English and Afrikaans, with the native languages only allowed to be used for subjects like art and music. The government's goal was to make sure that all black people in South Africa knew how to communicate with white people in "white" languages. There were widespread and at times violent protests against this, as many students didn't want to speak Afrikaans. There were strikes and boycotts of schools throughout the townships.

5   http://www.saha.org.za/imagesofdefinace/education_charter_campaign_transvaal_launch_forward_to_a_peoples_education.htm

2.2 Contemporary Background

Multilingual colonial societies have an interesting side-effect when it comes to languages. Organising a society along racial lines – as in apartheid South Africa, with whites on the top and blacks on the bottom – and enforcing the language(s) of the minority ruling class means that the lower classes are forced by circumstance and by law to learn the colonisers' languages. But they also grow up speaking their own tribal language. In the case of the black characters in *Mother to Mother*, that language is Xhosa.

Language

The result of this structure, with black native languages forbidden from being taught in schools but being the main form of communication at home, is that the blacks grow up speaking at least three languages – a tribal mother tongue, English and Afrikaans – whereas the white ruling classes will usually be limited to speaking only the official "white" languages.

The fluid ease with which Mandisa and her family switch between these languages and the interesting way in which the languages interact with and influence each other are looked at in this study guide in the chapter on *Style and Language* (p. 114).

The **quality of teaching** was also an issue. Over 90% of all the teachers in white schools were properly trained and certified teachers[6] whereas only about 15% of the teachers in black schools were trained teachers. The pass rate for exams and graduating among black students was less than half what it was for white students.

---

6   Information comes from the 1997 Library of Congress study: https://www.loc.gov/resource/
    frdcstdy.southafricacount00byrn

2.2   Contemporary Background

Segregated
education

The **issue of education** is very important in *Mother to Mother* –
Mandisa talks about it on pages 71–72, for example – but more
as a matter of context and environment. It is another one of those
outside influences contributing to the violence and unrest of the society and more specifically to Mxolisi's development and behaviour
as a young man. The generally low quality and restrictive nature
of segregated education in the apartheid state had the effect of increasing **ignorance, unemployment and despair** throughout the
black population. With no real education – we can see how Mandisa
is constantly frustrated in her efforts to educate herself – people
have no chance to get well-paying jobs or to improve their position
within society. The lack of perspectives creates more despair and
frustration, on the one hand: and on the other hand, **it provokes
radical and at times violent resistance and protest**.

The student protests

The school boycott was sparked by the deteriorating quality of education in black schools, the school age limit of twenty, and the policy that denied students representation by a democratically elected
Student Representative Council.[7]

The student protests of the "Young Lions" in 1993 which Mandisa
talks about were part of a **long tradition of protest and resistance**,
but in this year they were particularly energized by the frustratingly
slow pace of change and improvement in society and politics following the release of Mandela, among other developments. Mandela
had called the Young Lions "the government-in-waiting"[8] because
so many of their leaders were gifted, intelligent and energetic individuals who spoke passionately and articulately about **the need for**

---

7   http://ro.ecu.edu.au/cgi/viewcontent.cgi?article=1721&context=theses_hons
8   https://www.washingtonpost.com/archive/politics/1993/04/18/young-lions-eager-to-roar-in-s-
     africa/bdf3ed25-d83c-46e9-aeeb-e2430645c211/?utm_term=.1daa4a12e006

2.2 Contemporary Background

change in South Africa and an end to the oppression of the blacks. But many of these young people had come out of a nation-wide movement which had boycotted schools, protesting the state-led efforts to keep the black population in a state of passivity and ignorance.

While many of these young people wanted to become lawyers or politicians and active, professional members of society, most of them had little or no official education. Mandisa first mentions the student protests and education boycotts on page 10, describing how a student organisation (COSAS) told students to boycott schools out of solidarity with striking teachers. For Mandisa, this playing at politics and social unrest is unreal, **a dangerous and stupid game** which is stopping the young people from understanding life – as she sees it, by wasting their youth and not going to school, they all but guaranteeing that their lives as adults will be no better than her generation's: "if they're not careful, they'll end up in the kitchens and gardens of white homes … just like us, their mothers and fathers" (p. 10).

Education boycotts

2.3 Notes on Other Important Works

SUMMARY

Sindiwe Magona has written a two-volume autobiography (the first part of which was her first published work), a biography of Archbishop Ndungane, as well as short story collections, poetry and novels. She has also written more than 100 books for children – we won't be looking at these in this study guide, however.

Novels

The novels

PUBLICATION DATE	TITLE
1998	*Mother to Mother*
2006	*The Best Meal Ever*
2008	*Beauty's Gift*

Mother to Mother was Magona's first published novel, and it remains her most famous and successful work. ***The Best Meal Ever*** is set in a South African township and is about a girl having to look after her younger siblings. ***Beauty's Gift*** is a novel about a group of women and how they deal with the HIV/AIDS-related death of one of their circle of friends.

Short stories

Short story collections

PUBLICATION DATE	TITLE
1991	*Living, Loving and Lying Awake at Night*
1996	*Push-push! And Other Stories*

2.3   Notes on Other Important Works

As with her novels, **Magona's short stories** draw on her personal experiences and are all concerned with South African social issues, in particular those affecting women.

Poetry

PUBLICATION DATE	TITLE
2009	*Please, Take Photographs*

Autobiographies

PUBLICATION DATE	TITLE
1990	*To My Children's Children*
1992	*Forced to Grow*

To My Children's Children, Magona's first published work, is an open letter to her grandchildren in which she tells the story of her own life up to the age of 23, and shares what she can of Xhosa culture and traditions. She presents herself explicitly as a "Xhosa grandmother", and the book is of interest as a personal memoir, as an eyewitness account of the apartheid era, as an anthropological study of Xhosa tribal customs and folklore, and as a study of how women of all ages suffer and are oppressed under patriarchal social systems. *Forced to Grow* continues her autobiography from the age of 23 on.

Biography

PUBLICATION DATE	TITLE
2012	*From Robben Island to Bishop's Court*

2.3 Notes on Other Important Works

This is **a biography of Archbishop Njongonkulu Ndungane**, who was a pioneering anti-apartheid activist who was imprisoned on Robben Island, where Nelson Mandela also spent many years in prison. After being released from jail he continued to work to end apartheid, and campaigned for the rights of HIV positive people, equal rights for women and protecting the poor and dispossessed.

Children's books

Children's books

PUBLICATION DATE	TITLE
Not yet published	*The Stranger and His Flute,*
	Greedy Man, Kind Rock
	Nokulunga, Mother of Goodness
	Stronger Than Lion
	Buhle, the Calf of Many Colours
	The Woman on the Moon

Magona has written more than 100 books for children over the years. This forthcoming series of books[9] for children will be published in four South African languages as well as in English. These tales are intended by Magona **to promote reading** in general – she worries that South Africa lacks a culture of reading – as well as supporting and promoting literacy in African languages.

---

9   http://sindiwemagona.wixsite.com/website/upcomingbooks

3. ANALYSES AND INTERPRETATIONS

3.1 Origins and Sources

SUMMARY

Mother to Mother is a fictionalised account of the murder in August 1993 of American student Amy Biehl in the South African township of Gugulethu (Guguletu in the novel, also known as Guguleto). It draws heavily on author Sindiwe Magona's own life: she was born in Gugululu, lived in Guguletu, worked as a maid in white family's homes, and lived through the apartheid era and its aftermath.

Guguletu

Mandisa describes the township (see pp. 27–34, for example) as she experienced it, having been forced to move there with her family when she was 10, and talks about the mistakes that had been made in how it was set up – mistakes that range from the evil to the incompetent.

The name Guguletu is a shortened form of the Xhosa phrase "igugu lethu", which means "our pride" – a name which acquires a particularly **bitter irony**, both historically and in the fictional context of the novel. The township was established in the 1960s and was infamous for its high levels of unrest and crime. As presented in the novel, it is a crowded place with high unemployment, a lot of poverty and social neglect, and an intimidating, militarised police presence. Mandisa describes a **depressing environment** with little support for young people, who are left to wander the streets feeling frustrated and neglected. As well as being the site of the actual murder of Amy Biehl in 1993, Guguletu is a microcosm of

"Our pride"

3.1 Origins and Sources

South Africa's racial and social troubles, and for this reason it is one of the most significant original inspirations for the novel. With its extraordinarily high levels of violent crime and racially segregated, socially troubled population, the township provides a grimly ideal setting for the author's intentions, as outlined in her preface, to look at what lessons can be learned from a tragedy like the murder of Amy Biehl, and to more closely examine the failures of a society which is corrupted by injustice and brutality.

The author Sindiwe Magona grew up in Guguletu, and she would have seen and experienced the apartheid era in its entirety. Her familiarity with the township is evident in her strong evocation of its history and chaotic life.

The murder of Amy Biehl

Athol Fugard says he was sickened last summer when he learned of **the murder of Amy Elizabeth Biehl**, the white Fulbright scholar from Newport Beach who was pulled from her car and stabbed by a mob screaming anti-white slogans in the black township of Guguleto, South Africa.

"Her death was horrible, awful," he said, recalling that the idealistic, 26-year-old Biehl had been studying the role of women during South Africa's current political changes.

"The slogan that crowd was chanting–'One settler! One bullet!'–is one of the bitter fruits of apartheid. It's not just the young men who are chanting it, you know, but the young women as well."

3.1 Origins and Sources

> Nevertheless, Fugard adds, white South Africa bears as much responsibility for Biehl's death as the black youths who actually wielded the murder weapons and shouted the slogans. "That violence and that rage were created by the system," he said.
> "I'm not absolving those young people of responsibility. But I would be so blind, I would be guilty of such terrible complacency if I didn't acknowledge that it is the system of white privilege and white domination that created two generations of lost young men and women for whom violence is the only way forward, as they see it."[10]

Amy Biehl (1967–1993) was a white US American student who was **killed by a mob of black South Africans in Guguletu**. Four men were convicted of the murder, but their convictions were later overturned and they were freed by the post-apartheid Truth and Reconciliation Commission.

Amy Biehl had been a student at Stanford University (USA) and was studying at the University of the Western Cape on a scholarship from the Fulbright Program. She was an anti-apartheid activist and, as shown in the novel, she was **friends with black students**. The account of her death in *Mother to Mother* is largely accurate: she had offered to drive black friends back home to Guguletu, where an already-active mob of black youths spotted her and stabbed and stoned her to death.

Student and anti-apartheid activist

As Sindiwe Magona points out in her preface to the novel (pp. v–vi), there is an irony, however morbid, in Amy having been

---

10 http://articles.latimes.com/1994-01-27/news/ol-16092_1_amy-biehl

3.1 Origins and Sources

killed by precisely the people she was most trying to help. Her stated aim in writing the novel is **to present the world which produced Mxolisi** (who here stands as a fictional representative of the four convicted killers), and by doing so to attempt to show and explain how the dehumanising brutality and injustice of the apartheid system made the young black population of South Africa capable of such **violent and destructive impulses.**

Amy Biehl's murder was one of the most high profile cases in South African history. Although many white tourists have been killed over the years while in the country, something about the Biehl case resonated far beyond the usual limits of shock, outrage and grief. This is probably not due simply to the fact that a young white American girl was murdered by black African men, but rather to the anti-apartheid, **politically and socially active role** she had been playing in the country prior to her death. As Nelson Mandela mentioned in his speech accepting the Congressional Gold Medal[11], Amy Biehl "made our aspirations her own" – she was working actively towards achieving **the dreams of a free and just society in South Africa**, liberated of racist government oppression and strong enough to tackle the post-apartheid turmoil.

Amnesty for Amy's killers

Amy Biehl has, since her death, been held up as an example of conscience-driven social activism. Her father welcomed the amnesty granted to her killers in the **spirit of forgiveness and understanding**, and he and her mother have founded a Foundation Trust to benefit township youths.[12]

---

11 http://www.americanrhetoric.com/speeches/nelsonmandelacongressionalgoldmedalspeech.htm
12 https://www.sahistory.org.za/dated-event/amy-biehl039s-murderers-receive-amnesty-trc

3.1 Origins and Sources

Police

> "When have the Guguletu Police been known for being reason-
> able, to say nothing of polite? Courteous? HA! Don't make me
> laugh." (Mandisa, p. 164)

As the most visible and present face of an oppressive regime, the police appear in *Mother to Mother* in a very negative light. We see them
rampaging through Mandisa's family's house, murdering suspects,
and lurking in their fortress-like stations with the fearsome 6-wheel
armoured Saracens[13] intimidating the locals. They are **something
to be feared** and avoided at all costs: very far from the "friend and
helper" of Germany, or from the "protect and serve" ideal of the
USA. As a group they are frightening and menacing, and individual
police officers appearing in the novel only reinforce this impression.
For black residents of the townships, white police officers provide
no security and protection.

The South African
police grant no
protection and no
safety

   As one of the enforcement agencies of the white supremacist
apartheid regime, the police force in South Africa is shown here
to be still riddled with a **violent and racist approach** to policing
which considers blacks to be beneath the law, and grants them fewer
rights. A key scene in the long history of Mandisa and Mxolisi is
the incident when Mxolisi was 4 years old, and saw police officers
shoot and kill two boys after he told the police where they were
hiding (pp. 146–148). The incident traumatises Mxolisi for years
to come and obviously shapes his attitude towards white people,
authorities, the police and life in general. Another pivotal incident
also concerns the police, when they storm into Mandisa's house in
search of Mxolisi (Chapter 6).

---

13 https://www.globalsecurity.org/military/world/europe/saracen.htm

3.1   Origins and Sources

Henchmen of the apartheid system

The violence and racism of the white police is a major influence on the world presented in *Mother to Mother* – the police stand for the brutal racism of apartheid, a crushing and very real presence in the lives of the black population.

The author's life and experiences

Semi-autobiographical novel

To summarise these points which are raised in this chapter and elsewhere in this study guide, *Mother to Mother* draws heavily on the author's own life and experiences, but is far from being an autobiography. Sindiwe Magona is a writer who is **motivated by social awareness** and a moral and activist sense of what is important and what is right. The novel reflects this approach by tackling a real-life crime (the murder of Amy Biehl) which was the product of historical, social and political forces, movements and crimes – but not as crime fiction or as a drama about the tragedy of the girl's death, but instead as **a portrait of the world and history** which made it possible.

To make this real, convincing and truthful, the author draws on her own life. Like Mandisa, Sindiwe Magona:

→ Lived as a black woman in South Africa under apartheid
→ Was born in Gungululu
→ Grew up in Gugulethu
→ Became a mother at a young age (Magona was 19, Mandisa 15)
→ Was abandoned by the husband of her first child
→ Was a gifted student and wanted to study and educate herself
→ Worked as a maid in the homes of rich white families

3.2 Summaries

SUMMARY

The narrative is divided into chapters of differing lengths. Unusually, the chapters are not uniformly labelled. Some are numbered, some are identified by very specific dates and times, and then chapter one, for example, has a more poetic title. The chapters with no title other than their sequential number are primarily but not exclusively concerned with the past – with Mandisa's memories of childhood and her youth and the background of her family, her original home in Blouvlei and her new life in the township of Guguletu, and the social and political disturbances and developments in South Africa.

The specifically dated chapters cover the events of 1993 surrounding the death of the white girl in Guguletu. Some chapters are subdivided with specific times of day (for example, chapters 4 and 5).

1 - Mandisa's Lament (p. 1)

Mandisa addresses the mother of the white American girl her son has killed. She is not surprised her son (whom she describes as a monster) has killed someone. She is angry at the girl for having been in the wrong part of town (Guguletu), and angry at the government in South Africa for only feeding and caring for her son now that he is in jail but for having left him hungry and wild before. She begs God to forgive her son.

Letter to the mother of the dead American girl

3.2 Summaries

2 - Mowbray – Wednesday 25 August 1993 (p. 5)

Mandisa imagines the dead American girl waking up in the morning in the district of Mowbray, and imagines what her life is like. She then describes her own family's morning as she wakes her children and talks to them briefly before she has to leave the house for work. She regrets having to work so much because she hardly ever sees her children and doesn't know what they do with their time.

Girl says goodbye to her African friends

She then imagines the white girl driving to school on the last day of her ten months spent here, and thinks about how busy she must have been. She thinks that the girl must have been excited, happy and sad to be returning home and saying goodbye to the friends she has made here.

She worries about her son's laziness and lack of direction, and about how poorly educated and guided her children (and other children in the country) are. Mxolisi leaves home and joins a rapidly growing group of other young black men out on the streets of which he is the leader.

She imagines the white girl meeting with her friends in the university cafeteria. Finding it hard to say goodbye, she offers to drive three of the African girls from Guguletu home. They are sceptical because she is white, but she insists. They set off in the car – the white girl, her three black girlfriends, and another boy who lives near her and will drive back with her to Mowbray.

Mxolisi's group is trying to find a large enough room for them all to meet, but they are being refused entry to schools, churches and other meeting places. They decide to meet the next morning at the church in Guguletu. The large group disperses as the boys head off home. On his way home, Mxolisi and his friends see a delivery truck in flames. When they hear police sirens they flee, worried about being shot or arrested if they are seen near the fire. The group meets up with others from earlier, and then heads off

3.2 Summaries

again, separating into ever-smaller groups. Mxolisi and his friends are heading towards the police station in Guguletu.

The white girl and her friends get into her car and drive off, getting on to the highway and heading for Guguletu.

Mxolisi and his friends see the police station but are scared and head off home. The white girl's car approaches. Mxolisi, leaving for home, hears a commotion and returns to look: he sees the girl's car, surrounded by an angry mob.

3 - 5.15 pm – Wednesday 25 August 1993 (p. 20)

This chapter includes a brief history of Guguletu and descriptions of its current state. Mandisa's recollections of arriving in Guguletu describe how and why the slums were created, the neglect and mistakes of its establishment, and the human consequences of those errors.

History of Guguletu

Mandisa is at work at Mrs Nelson's when the white woman tells her that her work for the day is done and she'll take her back to the bus station now. She is in a hurry and seems panicked. She says that there is trouble in Guguletu. When they get to the bus station they find chaos. There are rumours there too that there is big trouble in Guguletu (which is briefly described by Mandisa as she recalls having arrived there in 1968 with her family when she was 10 years old).

A young man on the bus says that he was there and saw what happened: Locals attacked and set alight a car full of university students. When the bus finally gets to Guguletu and stops near the police station, Mandisa is caught up in a crushing crowd as she fights to get home. Her daughter is waiting there for her.

4 - 7.30 pm (p. 40)

Siziwe and Lunga are at home, Mandisa learns, but Mxolisi is not. Mandisa thinks of the differences between her oldest child and the younger kids.

7.45 pm

A white women was killed

Skonana, Mandisa's neighbour, is eager to talk. She tells Mandisa that a white woman has been killed by local children. Mandisa is shocked at the news – the killing of a white woman, she understands, will cause immense trouble for the township. Skonana tells her that the white woman had been killed right here on the street where they live, and that she had been stabbed.

5 (p. 48)

> This lengthy and important chapter covers both the present day (1993) and Mandisa's childhood, moving back and forth between the times, and looks in some depth at the origins of the troubles in Guguletu, particularly the failure of the education system.

Relocation in townships

Mandisa cannot understand why anyone (specifically the white woman who has been killed) would voluntarily come to Guguletu. She remembers her childhood before her family was relocated to Guguletu, and how happy and (relatively) carefree it had been. She thinks of the sense of community, tradition and family bonds that are now missing, in the context of remembering when and how the news of the relocations surfaced and spread. Nobody believes that the rumours are true: Everyone in Blouvlei feels secure and at home. They feel deeply connected to the land beneath the tin shacks

)

3.2 Summaries

they built themselves. This is their home. Later in the year, when the rumour has been largely forgotten, the government begins the relocations.

Mandisa is playing outside with her friends when an aeroplane flies over Blouvlei and dumps thousands of flyers informing the inhabitants that they will be relocated next month. Everyone is alarmed by the message and a gathering of adults is called at the meeting place in Blouvlei. There are many questions but no answers, and after weeks of meetings and discussions, the government refuses to respond or answer the township's questions.

The relocations are postponed from July and begin before dawn on the first of September. White people come into the township and begin tearing down the shacks. Blouvlei is surrounded by police and the army, and hundreds of white men start tearing the dwellings to pieces with their hands. They ignore all resistance. Mandisa's parents, seeing that resistance is futile, tear down their own home and try to salvage as much of the building materials as they can, even rusty old nails and pieces of cardboard. The people of Blouvlei are escorted by the government to the site of their new home: A wilderness with ugly concrete houses. Mandisa remembers that very soon all the mothers had to work, mostly in the homes of white women, and were no longer at home to look after the children, and that soon, she couldn't even remember what it was like to be welcomed home with a smile by her own mother.

10.05 PM – Wednesday 25 August 1993

Mandisa is waiting for Mxolisi to come home. Her husband comes first, with some meat for dinner, but she waits and waits to serve the food because she is anxious about her son. He has still not returned by the time Mandisa is ready to go to bed. Mandisa is sick with worry about her son but also about the consequences of a

Mxolisi is missing

3.2   Summaries

Violent youth protests in a Johannesburg township in 2017.
© picture alliance/ AP Photo

white woman having been killed – the violence in itself is not surprising.

She remembers how white people who try to help the blacks in South Africa are treated, or have been treated in the past, recalling a specific example of three Belgian nurses who were beaten by a mob of African men when they were trying to monitor government oppression and abuse.

Bad school system

Dwadwa inquires that night about Mxolisi and warns Mandisa that the boy will cause great trouble. She tries to defend him. Unable to sleep, Mandisa lies in bed and thinks about her childhood again. She remembers how the school she went to in Guguletu was so overcrowded that by the end of the first year she didn't even know

3.2 Summaries

the names of all the children in her class. The education system had been bad when she was a child, but had become worse and worse over time, until there were student riots in 1976 to protest the terrible state of education for blacks. Mxolisi is 20 but is in a class for 12-year olds – and Mandisa thinks that he is not even the oldest child in that class. She thinks that a combination of "boycotts, strikes and indifference" (p. 72) have damaged the schools over the past 20 years, and that it is the children who suffer the most.

In a brief interruption of the narrative (p. 72), Mandisa again directly addresses the mother of the dead white girl, asking her why, with all the education she must have had, the girl had not known enough to stay away from Guguletu.

Mandisa worries about the breaking of bonds between parents and children, and how uncontrollable the children have become in the townships. She remembers in her own childhood having been taught a song about the killing of a white nun by Africans in East London, and wonders how things have become the way they are. She thinks about the progression of violence and resistance from throwing stones at white people's cars to burning white people's buildings – and from there to attacking black-owned cars and homes. Mandisa is thinking about the combination of poor education with political violence, and she compares the behaviour of the violent youth movements with the manipulation of fear and anger practiced by witch-doctors when identifying a witch for punishment by the community. She sees that the younger generations have turned their frustration and anger against their own communities, their own parents. She sees it as a descent into barbarism, finding its horrific crescendo in the use of the "necklace" to kill people (a tire put around the victim's neck, filled with petrol and set alight). This awful way of killing is described as being revolutionary, and Mandisa says that the "children" (p. 77) claim that they are using

War in the townships

3.2   Summaries

it to fight the apartheid government – but it is not the oppressors who are being killed, only other blacks from the townships.

6 - 4 am – Thursday 28 August 1993 (p. 79)

Violent police

Mandisa awakes after a restless night with little sleep. She has been woken by the sound of a car door closing, and suddenly her house is surrounded by people beating on the doors and windows. It is the police. They force their way into the house and brutally mishandle Mandisa. The police demand to know where Mxolisi is. They search the house thoroughly for any clues, destroying furniture and dismantling the hut where Mandisa's boys sleep. They beat up Lunga.

7 (p. 88)

This chapter begins with a short direct address to the mother of the white girl.

Mandisa talks about Mxolisi, and how his birth in 1973 – when she was 15 – changed her life. She felt that things had begun to change for the worse already in 1971, when she began menstruating and her mother began worrying that she would become pregnant, and then in 1972 she discovered that her best friend Nono had been secretly having a relationship with her brother.

Mandisa meets
Stella

In 1973 she is fourteen and on an errand in the white district of Claremont. She encounters her old school friend Stella, who lives in a part of Guguletu where many others from Blouvlei have settled. Stella appears worldly (she smokes) and has an endless stream of gossip about other girls their age, and how many of them are now pregnant or married. Her news is all bad (a "litany of disasters") and

3.2   Summaries

Mandisa finds it depressing. Stella remembers as well that Sis'Lulu
has died. Mandisa is heartbroken at this news.

She and Nono mend their friendship and a handsome new boy
at school, China, becomes Mandisa's boyfriend. Mandisa's mother
constantly warns her not to have anything to do with boys or else
she will become pregnant, but Mandisa has received no kind of sex
education and doesn't quite understand what her mother means.
Her mother regularly inspects her genitals to make sure she is still
a virgin, a practice Mandisa finds humiliating.

In March of that year a classmate of Mandisa's dies during an
illegal back-yard abortion. In June Nono's mother Manono comes
to tell Mandisa's mother that her daughter is pregnant by Khaya
(p. 97). Manono curses Khaya and his entire clan. Mandisa's mother
is so upset by the fear of her own daughter getting pregnant that
she sends Mandisa off to the village where she grew up, Gungululu,
where she will live with her grandmother Makhulu, whom she has
never met.

*Nono is pregnant
by Khaya*

Gungululu – September 1972

Mandisa has been in the village for three months. Her grandmother
Makhulu cares for her but she is lonely and misses China, with
whom she feels deeply in love, and she feels abandoned by her own
mother.

One day after school Mandisa and Makhulu learn that Funiwe,
Mandisa's aunt, is coming from East London, and that she is pregnant and wants to have her baby in the village. Makhulu is delighted
and energised by the news. Mandisa decides that night that after
Funiwe's baby is born, she would like to return with her aunt to
East London and go to school there, where she could also offer to
help with the baby. She writes to China and asks him to arrange to
attend school near where she hopes she will be.

*Mandisa's plans
for next year*

3.2 Summaries

On the final day of school in Gungululu, Mandisa is named the second best student in her class. On the way home from the ceremony she finds she has a letter from China at the post office.

Mandisa is pregnant

Mandisa's aunt Funiwe arrives that night. Mandisa overhears her grandmother and aunt talking about her: Funiwe is convinced that the girl is pregnant. Mandisa only then realizes that she hasn't had her period for three months. The grandmother is shocked, and the two women interrogate the girl. Mandisa is shocked herself, admitting that she has a boyfriend but maintaining that she has done "nothing shameful" (p. 119). She tells them that her mother had never educated her about sex, but that her boyfriend had known what to do and how to be careful. She tells them who it is, and that he lives in Cape Town. The village midwife is summoned and she confirms that the girl is pregnant: but she appears to be still a virgin. Her mother is sent for and reacts hysterically, claiming that the shame will kill her. Funiwe points out that Mandisa has done nothing wrong and that it is a "sad accident" (p. 113). Mandisa is upset by her mother's reaction and feels fear, shame and anger.

Mandisa must now abandon her plans to move to East London with her aunt. She has to go back to Cape Town where she will be pregnant and have a baby, and the fact of her virginity and innocence provides no consolation. She feels that her life so far has come to a crashing halt and that everything now will change.

3.2   Summaries

8 (p. 115)

> This lengthy chapter focuses on the past, specifically Mandisa's life from the confirmation of her pregnancy to the birth of her third child, Siziwe. In covering this period of her life the reader is also shown more of Mxolisi and his development as a child.

A week after the village midwife had confirmed her pregnancy, Mandisa returns to Cape Town with her mother, where she finds that she has become "a prisoner in my home" (p. 117). Her mother even takes time off work to be able to monitor her all day long and doesn't go to church on Sunday. Her father ignores her completely. She is of course forbidden to have any contact with China, and her mother tells her that her father and uncles will be going to see China's father to discuss "payment of damages" (p. 119).

Back in Cape Town

Mandisa has just sent a secret message to China when he comes to the house to see her. When he sees that she is pregnant and she tries to talk to him, he is cold and angry and refuses to accept that he is the father. He tells her he wants to go to boarding school to get a better education, and seems more interested in his future plans than in the pregnancy. She is furious at his self-involvement and refusal to accept responsibility, and she chases him out of the house.

Sad meeting with China

Six months into her pregnancy, Mandisa is taken by her uncles to China's house to discuss the situation with China's family. China's relatives are surprised by the news that Mandisa is still technically a virgin, and although they don't refuse to accept responsibility, they say that they will get back in touch once they have talked within the clan.

3.2   Summaries

Mandisa's son is born

Eight months into the pregnancy, a white priest commands China to marry Mandisa. Before they can marry, however, China has to be circumcised, and leaves to spend a month out in the bush. Mandisa gives birth before they can marry.

The negotiations with China's family are difficult and lengthy. Two months after the birth, Mandisa no longer wants to marry China, but her parents insist. She feels nothing but contempt for him now, considering him vain and cowardly. Mandisa argues that it is too late now to save face by marrying the father of her child, and that a forced marriage would make them both extremely unhappy. Her father takes her side in the argument and agrees that she can continue with her education, and that she needn't marry China – but the larger family decides otherwise and rules that she won't be going back to school.

Mandisa and China have to marry

Three weeks later Mandisa marries China. There is no ceremony, and the marriage is simply an arrangement between the two families. Mandisa has to leave her home. When the time comes, her mother is sad, and she realises that her mother has grown to love the baby. Mandisa feels that she has been forced to abandon all her hopes and dreams now that she has to marry China.

Mxolisi – "will bring peace"

At her new home, where she and China will live with China's aunt, Mandisa has to undergo a ritual of naming. Her new family chooses a new name for her ("the name of wifehood"), as well as a name for the child. The family decides on the name Mxolisi ("he who will bring peace"; p. 136).

Mandisa had not wanted to marry China at all by this point, and she was forced into it by her family and his. She is shocked and upset by the renaming of her baby. The marriage begins badly, with the couple arguing and ignoring one another. China begins working at a meat storage company, and is always very tired and unhappy. But Mandisa's days are even longer and she is constantly exhausted

3.2 Summaries

and loses a lot of weight. The difference between them is not only that Mandisa works harder and longer than China, but that he is getting paid for his work and she isn't for hers.

Mandisa very much wants to go back to school to continue her education, and was promised during the marriage negotiations that she would be able to, but China's family delay and postpone and eventually deny her this. And then China abruptly leaves shortly after Mxolisi's second birthday: Mandisa never sees him again. China's family searches for him but can't find him. His father stops visiting the house, meaning there is even less money to go around, and so Mandisa has to get a job as a domestic servant. She rents a room elsewhere and moves out together with her baby.

China leaves the family

Mxolisi grows and develops astoundingly fast. Mandisa understands that he misses both his father and his grandfather, who has by now completely left their lives. When he is four years old, the police come to the house where Mandisa and Mxolisi live – a hut in the backyard of a larger house. Mxolisi has become friends with the two boys from the family in the big house, who are older than him. When the boys hide and the police search for them, Mxolisi points to where they are hiding, thinking it's a game, and the police shoot the two boys dead. Mxolisi doesn't speak again for another two years. He is deeply and lastingly traumatised by the incident.

Traumatic event for Mxolisi

Doctors in a hospital can't help, so after six months Mandisa takes her son to see a faith healer (sangoma). She tells Mandisa that she must love her son, that resentment can be worse than hate, and she commiserates with Mxolisi, telling the boy that he must bear too much responsibility for his young age.

Mandisa meets a man named Lungile at Khaya and Nono's wedding and they become lovers, although they don't marry. She has a son by Lungile, called Lunga, and initially, Mxolisi reacts badly to the new baby. He is still not talking and he started wetting his

Mandisa's second baby Lunga is born

3.2   Summaries

bed. But then suddenly one day, after not having said a word for two years, he asks Mandisa where his own father is (p. 159).

After this moment he apparently improves. He never speaks of the two friends of his who were shot by the police, but Mandisa can see he carries the guilt with him.

Mandisa gives birth to her third child Siziwe

Mxolisi goes to school, where he is an excellent student, but he resents being disciplined. Lungile leaves South Africa to train as a freedom fighter, leaving Mandisa with two children, and Mxolisi quits school and gets a job. Mandisa desperately pleads with him to go back and eventually he does, going on to high school. But it is in high school where other problems start: Mxolisi becomes involved with politics. He becomes a popular leader amongst the radical students, demanding liberation and advocating violent resistance. He spends less and less time at home. Mandisa marries Dwadwa and gives birth to her third child, her daughter Siziwe.

Mxolisi has become something of a hero on the streets, and Mandisa is often congratulated by people who know of her son's activities. But she has less and less contact with or control over him. She tells of one instance where he had saved a girl from being raped, and two people who had seen this came to Mandisa's house to thank her for the goodness of her son. But now, she says, people like this treat her as if she herself had ordered her son to kill the white girl.

9 - 6 am Thursday 26 August (p. 164)

Shocked by the police raid

Back in the present day (1993): Mandisa and her family recover from the aggressive encounter with the police, and wonder what is going on with Mxolisi. Dwadwa and Lunga have both been hurt by the police and Siziwe is very upset, and appears to be in a state of deep trauma-induced shock. When the neighbours come to find out what has happened Dwadwa impatiently drives them away.

3.2 Summaries

Once Siziwe has recovered she tells Mandisa that Mxolisi had returned home that day before the police came, and that he had hidden something in his room. Siziwe is obviously concerned about whatever had happened, but she then goes silent and refuses to tell her mother anything else.

Dwadwa gets ready for work, Lunga goes to sleep before he has to go to school, and Mandisa is sad and angry and frightened for her son. She says she will go and look for Mxolisi if he doesn't return home, but Dwadwa reminds her that he had said the boy was destined to bring scandal and trouble on them.

10 (p. 173)

Mandisa remembers her grandfather Tatomkhulu teaching her about Xhosa history and traditions; at school she had only learned the history of the European colonists. He teaches her about an event in Xhosa history: In 1857, the people slaughtered all of their cattle and burned all their farmland in an attempt to drive the white settlers away. They had done this in hope of a kind of divine intervention, but nothing happened – the sun set in the West as usual, and the white settlers stayed, and the people began to starve and die. The white settlers then approached the Xhosa and offered to pay and feed them in return for their working in the mines.

1 pm – Thursday 26 August

Mandisa wakes up. Siziwe has made her breakfast and seems much recovered. She tells her mother that Lunga has gone – that boys with cars came to get him, and that they said something about Mxolisi. Siziwe becomes upset and tells her mother that she thinks it all has something to do with the death of the white girl the day before.

A priest comes to visit – Mfundisi Mananga. He is from the An-glican Church, and Mandisa is a Methodist, so she is surprised to

Day after the murder of the white woman

see him. The priest speaks loudly and in an unnatural voice, telling Mandisa that she should tell Mxolisi if she sees him that the priest has finally found a room large enough to host Mxolisi's meeting. While he is talking, however, he is scribbling a message for Mandisa on a scrap of paper. He seems to be extremely nervous. The note says that she should take a taxi to a specific location. Continuing to speak loudly about something completely different, the priest signals to her that she should keep silent and then leaves.

Mandisa meets Mxolisi at a secret location

When Mandisa gets into the taxi a girl makes contact with her, secretly passing her another note, this one telling her when to get out of the taxi. When she arrives at the destination the priest appears again in a car and gives her further directions. She ends up in a car with a beautiful, educated woman and a mysterious man who keeps his face hidden. They bring her to a house in another part of town: she doesn't know where she is. In the house are two men and a woman who say that they are just leaving. After half an hour of waiting, Mxolisi suddenly appears from somewhere else in the house.

Mxolisi is frightened

He admits to having been one of the crowd who threw stones at the car the white girl was in. She remembers that her neighbour told her that the girl had been stabbed: Mxolisi says many people stabbed her. When Mandisa asks him point-blank if he was one of them he refuses to answer. She asks him if it was him, his knife, which killed the girl, and he promises that it wasn't. But she sees in his eyes that he is truly terrified of what he has done and what has happened. She tries to find out from him why everyone – including the police – think that it was he who killed the girl. She tells him that it doesn't matter if he had only scratched the girl's thumb with his knife – if he has drawn her blood he will be charged with her murder. She can see only pain and terror in her son's eyes.

3.2 Summaries

11 (p. 198)

> Mandisa again addresses the dead girl's mother with questions about how she should feel and the tragedy of the girl's death.

Mandisa compares the two young people – the girl's fearlessness and bright future, and her son's desperate and doomed life. She is ashamed for his actions and furious at the people who led him to behave like this – the adults who used the children in the student protests and taught them how to be violent. She is in anguish at the two tragedies – the murder of the white girl and the tragedy of her son, and the deeper, wider tragedy of the hopelessness, violence and neglect of the culture which produced him and thousands of other young men just like him.

Mxolisi and the white girl

Guguletu, much later

Mandisa's neighbours come to her house to comfort her and grieve with her. She opens up and they talk. She draws strength from this support, this sense of community, and takes hope in the knowledge that on a larger scale similar things happen in the wider community: initiatives and groups working with young people, trying to help stop the violence and the causes of the violence.

She says to the other mother that she must feel no shame, that she should take comfort in knowing that she did everything she could for her daughter. There is the loss and grief, but no shame and no failure on her part.

3.2 Summaries

12 (p. 203)

Mandisa speaks about the futility of her son's life. He had already seen what his future held for him, the hopelessness of life for millions of people like him.

Guguletu, late afternoon, Wednesday 25 August

The murder of the white girl

Mandisa describes the events of the afternoon on which the girl died. She is driving her friends home, as arranged: Mxolisi and his group are separating now, tired and finished for the day. They see the car approaching but no one notices. It is only when the car stops at a traffic light that someone spots the white person in it, and suddenly the violence erupts, "ONE SETTLER! ONE BULLET!" (p. 205).

The crowd which had dispersed now reforms and the shouts attract more and more people. The girl tries to drive away but she is blocked in by other cars. The crowd begins to throw rocks at the car, breaking the window and hurting the people inside. They break out of the car and try to escape but it is hopeless.

Mandisa says that her son was just an agent – an agent of the dark angers of his race, hatred and resentment. She knows that he stabbed her, but understands that he was consumed by something much larger than himself. She sees the influence of chance on the encounter: A slight change in time and place would mean that the girl would still be alive, and that her son would not be a murderer – or at least, not yet.

4 CRITICAL
RECEPTION

5 MATERIALS

6 SAMPLE EXAM
QUESTIONS AND ANSWERS

3.3 Structure

3.3 Structure

SUMMARY

Mother to Mother is written from the first-person perspective. It is unusual in that the text directly addresses a second person as "you", referring to the mother of the murdered white girl. It is told from a point in time after the events of 1993, and the combination of memories and hindsight with the history, causes and consequences of social and political developments in South Africa makes it a very contemplative, introverted narrative. Large sections of the text concern Mandisa's introspection and memories.

Mandisa as narrator

Despite containing action, drama and moments of violence, the three major structural frames – the mother to mother appeal; the layers of memories and history; and the introspection and soul-searching of the narrator as she examines herself, her life, and the world that shaped her son – make the tone and feel of the novel more complex. To say that it lacks the fast, forward-pushing drive of an exciting thriller does not mean that the novel is boring or lacks energy. Rather, the narrator's sensitivity to the layers of memories and history means that the novel reaches outwards into the spaces around it, into the history of the country and the deep roots of the hatred and racial injustice in South Africa, to look more closely at **the context and environment which led to the killing of Amy Biehl**.

As the author states in her preface, her narrator, Mandisa, is drawing "a portrait of her son and of his world" (p. vi). As a portrait in the form of a novel, *Mother to Mother* has a fitting structure, one which looks deep into its subject and the history and space around it, rather than rushing from start to finish.

3.3 Structure

The narrative perspective – mother to mother

The narrative structure of the novel reflects the content, as made explicit by the title: one mother is directly addressing another. The framing narrative – the passages in italics scattered throughout the novel – is **the voice of Mandisa** talking to the mother of the dead white girl. While her voice may not be really talking to the woman, face to face, and may not represent a real written address to the grieving woman, for example in a letter – that is, even if the narrative "I" and what it says only exists on Mandisa's mind – she is nevertheless trying to explain herself and her son Mxolisi, and to investigate and understand and explain their history and the context of their lives and the world they have lived in.

Mandisa feels guilty for what has happened

Both mothers have suffered life-changing tragedy here, but Mandisa tries, towards the end of the novel, to explain why she thinks that the mother of the dead girl can take comfort in the knowledge that she did everything she could to give her daughter a good life and make her a strong person. The other mother, she argues, has no guilt and is not to blame for what has happened. The implication here, and something with which Mandisa struggles throughout the novel, is that she does feel guilty and does feel that she is to blame for what has happened. This issue is complex and is made more so by the social and historical conflicts which deform and batter the people of South Africa.

One sad lesson at the heart of *Mother to Mother* is that **being a black woman in apartheid South Africa** means that your own life can never really be free; the limits and oppression of a racist society and the restrictions of a patriarchal tribal culture have denied Mandisa the opportunity to become everything she is capable of – this is contrasted here with the white girl, who was given the opportunity to fully achieve her potential.

3.3 Structure

Layers of memories

The narrative has a kind of tidal ebb and flow quality to it, with the present-day events surging up to crisis points, while Mandisa's memories and histories of how and why this has all happened are retreating, both in time and in narrative urgency.

The layers of memories from her childhood and youth, and the associated histories of the settlements and society around her, are distinct in tone from the accounts of the events of 1993, but serve to illustrate **how things have become the way they are**. For example, following the intense and frightening chapter in which the police storm her house early in the morning in search of Mxolisi (pp. 79–86), the narrative withdraws into the past. For two lengthy chapters we go back to Mandisa's youth, but not to the point when she became pregnant with her firstborn child: it goes further back, to 1971, and then moves forward through her significant memories of 1971–1973, up to her banishment to live with her grandmother and the news of her pregnancy.

Mandisa's memories, the history and the society

Earlier, before the raid, Mandisa and Dwadwa had a conversation about Mxolisi's difficult nature (pp. 70–71) which led Mandisa, in a natural progression of thoughts, to think about the failing education system, the generation of desperate and violent "Young Lions" and the violence of the student protests, and her generation's responsibility and guilt. This is late at night, and soon after Mandisa finally falls asleep, she is woken by the sounds of the police preparing to invade her home. The police break in and raid her home, brutalising her family in search of Mxolisi, and then Mandisa's narrative escapes into the past.

So we have here **a progression of layers of time**:

→ from the present, with Mandisa and her husband discussing Mxolisi's problems and Mandisa reflecting on the wildness and violence of Mxolisi's generation,

3.3 Structure

→ into the "big picture" past, with a look at society and social and political developments, and the terrible, inhuman violence which has grown in this environment of hatred and oppression and the hopelessness and despair of Mxolisi's generation;

→ and then back to the present, with an intense and detailed description of a brutal police raid on her home, in search of Mxolisi;

→ and then back again into the past, but now it is the intimate, personal past of the narrator as a child, leading up through the history of her youth, her pregnancy, the birth of Mxolisi and her early years as a single mother of a troubled child to the aftermath of the police raid.

Black boys as monsters – white girls as victims

Everything about this sequence of chapters **(5, 6, 7 and 8)**, which form **the core of the novel**, is about Mxolisi and the effect he has had on the world. Symbolic of all "young black men", he is loved and unwanted, cared for and feared, neglected and disenfranchised, gifted and delinquent, suspected of the worst crimes and both guilty (he killed the girl) and innocent (he is the impotent product of his environment). The ambiguity, guilt, love and grief of the novel is all contained here in these central chapters, which are very much about how **the system of apartheid** has warped the lives of black people to create monsters in the boys and helpless victims in the girls.

The complexity of the story

There is very little about the story and the themes of the novel which has a black and white clarity – these issues are very complex. The way the narrative moves back and forth through time is symptomatic of this complexity. It is important to remember that there is nothing in this story which can be examined or presented in a vacuum, free of context or history; causes and influences on event and individuals have very complex roots which go far back

3.3 Structure

in time. The author is very careful to make sure the reader understands that **past events influence the present**, and that events of the present cannot be judged or evaluated without knowledge of the past.

Mandisa's narrative, moving back and forth from her childhood to the tragedy of 1993, reflects this **interconnected complexity of cause-and-effect** as well as being a necessary product of it.

Thoughts and memories – an introspective narrative

Much of the narrative involves **Mandisa's memories and thoughts**. It is very introspective. The framing structure of the narrative – Mandisa addressing the mother of the dead girl – requires Mandisa, as narrator, to examine her past, her relationship with her son, her feelings about what has happened, and to look at the influences and environment which made the crime possible.

Introspective

Mandisa must struggle with her identity: as a black person under the white supremacist state ideology of apartheid, as a daughter and a girl in a patriarchal and male-dominated society, and as someone who would like to study and get ahead in life, then suddenly becomes a parent (and a single parent on top of that) and feels as if **she has lost control of her life completely**. These issues of questioning and struggling with her identity continue through the various phases of motherhood, becoming a wife, neglecting her own children because she has to work as a maid for a white family somewhere else, and so on.

While the novel is full of "action" in the form of events, its substance largely consists of Mandisa's thoughts and feelings as she struggles to understand and come to terms with these events and the changes they bring about in her life. And because Mandisa grasps that **nothing happens in a vacuum** – that the events of her life have multiple, diverse origins and interconnections – her in-

3.3 Structure

ner narrative moves in a non-linear way, jumping backwards and forwards through time.

"Nothing would ever be the same for us." (p. 87)

When the police storm into the house in search of Mxolisi (pp. 79–87), everything changes. The signs were there before: Mandisa knows how troubled her son is, and how dangerous the situation is for restless young men in the townships. She also understood how dangerous things have become following the death of the white girl. But when the police come looking for Mxolisi, destroying her house and beating up her other son Lunga, she and her family enter **a new state of being**, completely separated from the life and the world they had known before.

The centre of the book

This is also of course **a pivotal moment in the narrative**, coming right in the centre of the book: There is a before and there is an after. This is a definitive point in the structure of the novel. Preceded by her reflections on her son's difficult nature and the violence of his generation, and followed by her own history and the history of her pregnancy and the birth of Mxolisi, this event is pivotal. As Mandisa says, "We could never go back to who we were before they had come." (p. 87)

3.3 Structure

TIMELINE

Chapter 1:
Mandisa's lament

Chapter 2:
The morning

5.15 pm **Chapter 3:**
The afternoon
Mandisa's way home
and the disturbances

7.30 pm **Chapter 4:**
7.45 pm Mandisa
learns about the death
of the white woman

10.05 pm **Chapter 5:**
Mandisa's conversation
with Dwadwa about
Mxolisi

Chapter 5:
Mandisa's childhood,
resettlement to Guguletu

7.30 am **Chapter 6:**
Police raid

Chapter 7:
Mandisa's pregnancy

Chapter 8:
Mxolisi's birth,
Mandisa's marriage and
separation. The deaths
of the neighbour's boys,
Mxolisi as a "hero"

6.00 pm **Chapter 9:**
After the raid

Chapter 10:
Mandisa's meeting with
Mxolisi

1.00 pm **Chapter 10:**
history/Xhosa

Later **Chapter 11:**
Mandisa's neighbours
visit her

Afternoon **Chapter 12:**
The death of the white
student

Mandisa's childhood
and youth

25th August 1993   26th August 1993

3.4 Characters

SUMMARY

The story is about an African boy, an American girl and their respective mothers. Mandisa narrates the story and her focus is very much on Mxolisi and the world around him: in telling the story of her life and her family, Mandisa is telling the story of how and why she thinks the American girl died. She and her son are the most important characters: He is at the centre of the plot, and she is telling the story.

Mandisa and her son Mxolisi

Two of the most important characters in *Mother to Mother* are not even present – the murdered white girl, who only appears in Mandisa's imagination, and the girl's mother, to whom the narrative is addressed. The central figures however are Mandisa, who tells the story in a first person narrative, and her eldest son Mxolisi, around whom the plot – and Mandisa's life – revolves.

One important factor here concerning the characters and their constellations is **the Xhosa family and clan system**. Mandisa is part of a family unit, until she has a child and becomes part of a new family unit, and each unit of family is part of a larger clan structure – in her case, the Chizama – which can include hundreds of other families, spread out across the country, and is itself part of a larger tribe, the Xhosa.

The Xhosa

Xhosa clan system – The Xhosa people are subdivided into clans or tribes. Some of these tribes are descended from intermarriages with white and/or Asian settlers and even castaways who landed on the South African coasts in the Middle

3.4 Characters

Ages (historical accounts and genetic analysis confirm some of these origin stories). The individual clans trace their ancestry back to one male ancestor, often a descendant of the founder of the race. For example, the ImiDushane clan was founded by Prince Mdushane in the 18th century, who was a son of King Ndlambe of the Rharhabe tribe and lived 1785–1819. Ndlambe in turn was one of King Phalo's five sons, most of whom founded a clan of their own. Phalo (died in 1775) is a direct descendent of Xhosa, the legendary (possibly mythical) founder of the Xhosa people, and the origin of the royal bloodline.

Xhosa clans, like most clan systems in different countries all around the world, are not only defined by territory, but more by family relations, language and traditions.

Mandisa

Mandisa, of the Chizama clan. Married name: Nohehake (p. 141). Mandisa is the narrator of the story; the novel is the story of her life leading up to and following the birth of her first child, Mxolisi, and covers the locations, events and times of **her life from childhood to the aftermath of the killing of the white girl**, in which her son was involved.

First person-narrator

Mandisa was born in 1958[14] in the village of Gungululu, where her grandmother still lives. She grew up in Blouvlei, a squatters' settlement in the Transkei region. She and her family were among those residents of Blouvlei who were forcibly driven out by a brutal

Born in Blouvlei

———

14   1993 is Mxolisi 20 years old. On his birth Mandisa was 15 years old.

3.4 Characters

joint operation involving the police and the military, and **forced to relocate to the township of Guguletu**, near Cape Town.

She marks 1972 as the year which "definitely delivered more than I had bargained for" (p. 88). Mandisa became pregnant in a freak accident – she remained technically a virgin – involving her boyfriend China. She was 15 at the time (in 1973), and the child was Mxolisi. She and China were **forced by their families to marry**, but China ran away, leaving her alone with a baby (p. 143). Mandisa was to have two more children by two different fathers.

Present day: 1993

By the year 1993 (which in *Mother to Mother* is the present day), Mandisa is living with her family in Guguletu and is working as a maid for a white family in Cape Town. Her husband Dwadwa, father of her youngest child, her daughter Siziwe, also works all day. She is unable to look after her own children as much as she would like, and only sees them briefly in the mornings and in the evenings.

She learns of the disturbances surrounding the killing of the white girl from her white employer, Mrs Nelson, and when she is back in Guguletu **her home is raided by the police**, who are looking for Mxolisi.

Mxolisi had been involved with youth gangs and anti-apartheid activist groups, and Mandisa is led by a series of activists to the place where her son is hiding from the police. He admits to having been involved in the white girl's death.

Hopes and dreams

Mandisa is **an ambitious, bright and strong-willed woman** whose expectations, hopes and dreams have been suffocated by the world around her. She intended to study when she was a girl, but her unwanted pregnancy at age 15 made this impossible. Two further pregnancies kept her in a state of perpetual motherhood, where she had to constantly work to keep her family going, and had less and less time and energy for herself.

3.4   Characters

Mandisa is **intelligent and reflective**, and she has few illusions now about life and other people ("Life is never problem free." p. 9). Her son's involvement in the death of the white girl forces her to re-examine her own life before and after the birth of Mxolisi, and she does so without self-pity.

An important part of her complex relationship with her family, her children and with Mxolisi in particular is the duty she feels to support them and the guilt she feels at being able to spend so little time with them (see for example p. 8). She feels that **she is not being the best mother she could be** because she is never there. She has to work so much that she can't supervise her children's daily lives and routines, make sure they go to school and do their homework, make sure they eat properly and at the right times. This guilt is caused by her sense of duty: **She has to work.** She has to earn money. Because Dwadwa, her husband, earns so little, she also has to make sure that the family has enough to survive. These important issues of motherhood, family and guilt are more closely examined in the chapter 3.5 Notes on Themes later in this study guide (see p. 108).

Mandisa feels guilty

Mandisa enjoyed her childhood in Blouvlei and is deeply upset by the family's forced relocation to the strange, unwelcoming and ugly township of Guguletu (see pp. 27–34, and in particular the first half of p. 33).

Naming conventions – Characters in the novel have many different names. This can be somewhat confusing for European readers at first. For example, Mandisa is born Mandisa; her white boss calls her Mandy (p. 20); China's family re-name her Nohehake when they marry (p. 134); and her grandfather

3.4   Characters

> calls her Mzukulwana (p. 174). Mxolisi is called Hlumeo,
> Michael, Bhabha, Boyboy and finally Mxolisi. Names have
> meanings – sometimes literal (Mzukulwana means grand-
> child) and sometimes figurative (Mxolisi means "he who will
> bring peace"). We see that individuals are given new names
> when they enter new phases of their lives – becoming a
> mother, a wife or a grandfather, for example.

Mandisa's children

Mxolisi

Mandisa's eldest son

He is 20 years old in 1993, but in school he is in Standard 6, which is the class intended for 12- or 13-year olds. Mandisa was 15 when he was born on January 4, 1973. His father was China (birth: p. 127). His birth name is Hlumeo (meaning sprig – a small twig with leaves on it), but Mandisa's mother insists on calling him Michael. Mandisa calls him Bhabha as a baby, and Boyboy as a child, but China's family, who have the traditional right to name babies, decides that his name will be Mxolisi, which means "he who will bring peace" (see pp. 134–136).

Leader of the young blacks in Guguletu

Mxolisi developed extremely quickly as a child (p. 145): as a young man he is "[g]iraffelike [...]. Tall and muscular" (p. 7). He is charismatic, and is popular amongst the other disaffected young men of Guguletu, who acknowledge him as one of their leaders. Mandisa is at times shocked when she hears his voice: "Some days Mxolisi sounds so much like his father I forget the years and think I will see China standing there when I raise my eyes." (p. 7) Mandisa becomes pregnant with Mxolisi in a freak accident, and remains technically a virgin. His birth changes everything for Mandisa: She

3.4 Characters

has to marry China – both her and his family insist – and she has to leave her family home to go and live with China at his aunt's home. China abandons her and the baby early on and she is left to raise Mxolisi by herself.

As a child, Mxolisi grows and develops with remarkable speed (p. 145). He can speak and walk and run much earlier than most children.

The discovery of Mandisa's pregnancy (pp. 109–114) is confusing and deeply upsetting for Mandisa and her family. Firstly, the fact that she is pregnant at all, despite not having had full intercourse with China, is a mystery which the village midwife in Gungululu tries to explain. Then there is the issue of her age – just 15 years old – and the fact that she and China are not married. Mxolisi's entrance into the world is complicated by confusion and difficult circumstances.

Despite that, however, Mandisa enjoys a secret happiness when she first feels her baby moving inside her: "But I was warm, all over [...] I couldn't hide the wide, wide smile in my heart." (p. 113) The birth is a torture, and Mandisa "hated [the baby] with a venom too fierce ever to die" (p. 127). When he is born and she first holds him, though, "I forgave him". She feels how her heart melts, "all pain forgot, all disappointment and bitterness, all grudges, everything negative, ablated. Joy, pure and simple…" (p. 127).

This ambiguous, increasingly difficult push-and-pull marks Mandisa's and Mxolisi's relationship throughout the novel – the tension between her love for her son and the trouble his mere existence causes her from the very beginning, not to mention the tragedy he later finds himself involved in. She feels that his existence has had a bad effect on her life: "A part of me hated him [...] the effect he seemed to have on my life. Always negative, always cheating

Mandisa and Mxolisi: ambivalent relationship

3.4 Characters

me of something I desperately wanted. I shrunk; because he was." (p. 142)

Mandisa is still herself half a child, and after China runs away and she takes Mxolisi and leaves China's family to live by herself, she and Mxolisi spend all their time together: she learns to play with him and takes him everywhere with her (p. 146). They have a very close bond.

Traumatic: Boys were shot

An extremely important incident in Mxolisi's life comes when the police kill two friends of his (pp. 146–148). He is a very young child, four years old, and thinks that his two friends are playing a game when they hide and the police come looking for them. Mxolisi tells the police where they are and the boys are shot. This is a **deeply traumatic event** in Mxolisi's life and he stops talking for more than two years.

Lungile and Mxolisi

Mandisa tries everything she can to get him to start talking again, but the doctors can't help, the sangoma (faith healer) she sees only gives her cryptic and emotional advice, and it is only when Lungile joins the efforts that Mxolisi suddenly start talking again, asking Mandisa who his real father is (p. 158). When Lungile leaves Mandisa to join up with freedom fighters in another country, Mxolisi quits school to get a job so he can help his mother. She persuades him to return to school frightened that he will otherwise become one of the "thousands upon thousands of young people who roam the township streets aimlessly day and night" (p. 161). But once back in school, he becomes involved in politics and the student boycotts – "serious problems started", says Mandisa (p. 161). He seems to his mother and her husband Dwadwa **to be ever more disobedient and difficult to control.**

Mxolisi is known in the neighbourhood for having rescued a girl from being raped (p. 60, pp. 162–163). "This boy of yours has a good heart", Mandisa is told by grateful neighbours. "There were

3.4 Characters

many people there. [...] None stopped the crime, none. Until your son arrived on the scene."

Mxolisi disappears after the girl is killed, and eventually Mandisa is led by a series of mysterious characters to where he is hiding.

"I should have such an obedient son!"
(Mandisa, p. 1)

Mxolisi's character and personality reflect the tension surrounding his conception and birth. He is a gifted and charismatic boy, **clever and intense**, a leader of his peers, a young man who can talk with adults and who has earned the respect of those who take him seriously. But he is also **a dangerous, violent, troubled boy**, someone who seems to attract trouble, and whose negative, hostile relationship with authority has been established at a very young age. He is lazy, disobedient and angry at the world. He bullies his younger brother and sister into doing his household chores.

Hostile relationship with the police

And yet he is affectionate, loving and loyal: Mandisa mentions that of all her children, he is still, as a troubled young man, "the most demonstrative" (p. 160), the most openly affectionate and emotional. When she first feels his presence within her, she is filled with love and happiness: "[...] I couldn't hide the wide, wide smile in my heart" (p. 113). She knows that she spoils him (pp. 35–36), and when she hears about the trouble in Guguletu in her neighbourhood, she prays "let my children be safe. Keep them safe, all of them ... but especially Mxolisi" (p. 36). She corrects herself instantly, saying she loves all of her children equally, but this slip shows the reader that the bond between Mandisa and her difficult, complicated firstborn son is particularly deep and intense. Even when she feels the fear that her daughter might be in danger of being raped if the trouble

Intense relationship with his mother Mandisa

3.4 Characters

spreads into a full-blown riot, she still thinks to herself, "deep down my heart, I knew I was more worried about Mxolisi" (p. 40). She tries to explain this to herself, thinking of the long period (6 years) the two of them were alone after China left, or the strange circumstances of his conception and birth – she acknowledges that **the bond between the two of them is different** from that which she shares with her other two children.

Mandisa is the narrator

This ambiguity is a major aspect of the novel. The complex interplay of the intense and troubled relationship between Mxolisi and his mother **is seen exclusively through her eyes** and forms one of the major arcs of development through her own life and through the story she is telling.

The most important event in Mxolisi's childhood is **the killing of his two friends by police**, which he thinks was his own fault (pp. 146–148). Mandisa believes that the trauma of this incident, which left him unable to speak for more than a year, deeply affected him and his relationship to the world.

Further influences on Mxolisi

Other factors which Mandisa believed impacted his development as a person include **the early disappearance of his father** (when he was two years old) and the subsequent **break from the rest of China's family**, especially China's father, Mxolisi's grandfather (p. 145), with whom the young boy had a good relationship. Mandisa sees that the little boy misses his grandfather. Mandisa knows that he is upset by the absence of his father, but he never mentions him until he is older. He is also negatively affected by **the birth of Lunga** when he (Mxolisi) is six years old (pp.157–159): he begins to wet his bed at nights, and then to ask about his own father, because he knows that Lungile is not his real father. This question – "Where is my own father?" (p. 159) – is the first thing he has said in almost two years, following the incident in which his friends were shot and killed by the police.

3.4 Characters

But beyond these deeply personal and specific events in his life, Mxolisi has been shaped by the **circumstances of his life and environment**. His mother is rarely there and he is free of all parental control. He has found an identity and a position of respect within the gang-like groups of students and young boys out on the streets (see p. 11 for a description of Mxolisi and the crowds of students). Like many boys of his generation and place in society, he feels – knows – that **he is unwanted by society**, unloved by family, that he is essentially nothing but an unwanted troublemaker. He hates the system which has created the unjust and brutal racist environment he lives in, and he is **active in protesting and rebelling** against it.

Life in a township in South Africa

An unwanted troublemaker

Lunga

Lunga is six years younger than Mxolisi. He is more obedient, causes less trouble, and is easier to wake up in the mornings (p. 7). Mandisa thinks he is "a bit on the soft side. Gentle" (p. 38). She compares her sons to different breeds of dog: Mxolisi is a pitbull, she says, meaning that he is fierce, strong, and dangerous, whereas Lunga is a dalmatian, implying that he is pretty but more or less harmless and lacking in aggression.

Son of Mandisa and Lungile

Siziwe

Siziwe is Mandisa's youngest child, her father is Dwadwa, Mandisa's current husband. She is obviously clever, and has more insight into Mandisa's difficult life and the problems and issues posed by Mxolisi than her mother would have wished – see for example the rich and detailed description of Siziwe's non-verbal reaction to her mother's concern about Mxolisi on page 41. This short but fascinating passage tells us a lot about:

Daughter of Mandisa and Dwadwa

3.4 Characters

→ Siziwe (her acute observation and intelligence, her pity for
her mother, tinged with contempt, are all on display in this
description of her facial expressions)
→ Mandisa (she feels naked before her daughter's understanding
of the way this family works and is disturbed by the pity and
contempt she feels)
→ Mxolisi (he is the acknowledged favourite, and his younger sister knows this)

Mandisa's husband and the fathers of her children

China

Mandisa's first
lover, father of
Mxolisi

They meet when Mandisa is 13 (p. 94) and he is a new student at
her school. A good-looking, bright and vain boy, Mandisa says he
is "Handsome as spring weather, and as popular" (p. 94). He is tall,
handsome and athletic (see description on p. 108). Mandisa was
completely infatuated with him during their early relationship ("The
thought of China lent me wings", p. 107), and even once she learns
that she is pregnant with his child. But his reaction to learning about
the pregnancy is just anger and denial (see pp. 121–124). Mandisa
thinks that he is "vain. Self-centred. And weak. He was a low-down
heartless cur" (p. 123). She later calls him a "lily-livered, spineless
dog, who shunned his responsibilities" (p. 129). The exposure of
his weakness and lack of sympathy, responsibility or feeling for
her is a great shock.

The young family has to live with China's aunt and struggles
to get by with very little money. China confirms Mandisa's bleak
analysis of his character by running away two weeks after Mxolisi's
second birthday (p. 143). Mandisa never sees him again.

As a character in the novel, China seems oddly unbalanced: He
is only present for a short period of time and doesn't do very much

3.4   Characters

(he's both lazy and a coward, we learn), but he has an **enormous
and lasting influence on Mandisa's life**. His son Mxolisi reminds
her of him, painfully (p. 7), but as a real figure he is long gone. China
represents one of many before-and-after moments in Mandisa's life:
The unexpected and unwanted event of her pregnancy turns her
overnight from a carefree girl with dreams of the future into a too-
young wife and mother with no future but serving her husband and
raising her child. As an equal partner in this new life, China fails
completely: too immature to help and too scared to try, he vanishes
from Mandisa's life, and from his son's as well.

Lungile

He is very short and powerfully built (p. 156) and not particularly
attractive. At the wedding of Khaya and Nono he makes repeated
efforts to get close to Mandisa, and insists on walking her home
afterwards. The relationship which develops has more to do with
Mandisa not wanting to be stuck with nothing in her life but Mxolisi
than it does with any love or great interest in Lungile: she makes it
very clear to him that they will not get married. They sleep together
that first night and Mandisa gets pregnant with her second child,
Lunga. The birth of the child is another **disturbing factor in Mxolisi's development**. Soon after Mxolisi goes back to school once
he has started talking again, Lungile leaves the country to train with
a group of freedom fighters, leaving Mandisa alone again, this time
with two children.

Mandisa meets
at the wedding of
Khaya and Nono

Lungile and Mxolisi get on very well together, which pleases
Mandisa, and she likes Lungile's sense of fun. He comes across as
a nice guy who, different from China, left **very little impression on
Mandisa's life** beyond giving her another child.

3.4 Characters

Dwadwa

Siziwe's father and Mandisa's husband

It's unclear how he entered Mandisa's life: "I now had three children, with the arrival of the girl, Siziwe. I had married Siziwe's father, Dwadwa" (p. 161).

Dwadwa is a reliable, calm man and a "good provider" (p. 68). He works hard (on the docks in Cape Town) and earns more than some, but not enough to support the family on just his income. He comes from the country and is an unsophisticated man, but he is "solid, steadfast, predictable" and Mandisa realises he is "exactly that type of man I wanted in my life" (p. 161).

He is frustrated with Mxolisi's behaviour and tells Mandisa: "mark my words, he will bring you a big trouble one day" (p. 71). He tries to be fair to all three of Mandisa's children, but he is angry when Mandisa claims that all the children are the same these days in their disobedience and secretiveness: Dwadwa tells her she is foolish, because he knows, as does Mandisa, that Mxolisi is a different kind of disobedient from Siziwe or Lunga.

Mandisa's extended family

Mama

Mandisa's mother

(girlhood name: Kukwana, p. 109) – She is a **strict woman**, and very concerned with the appearance of propriety – her response to learning that her unmarried, 15-year old daughter is pregnant is "What will the church people say? [...] What are they to think of me?" (p. 113). When Mandisa begins menstruating as a teenager her mother begins a humiliating ritual of physically examining her to make sure she is still a virgin (pp. 94–95), and she says to Mandisa: "Never let a boy come anywhere near you." (p. 94)

It is never really in doubt that she loves her daughter, but she refuses to take her seriously and to consider her feelings and de-

3.4 Characters

sires. Mandisa says of her mother, "not once did she indicate that she considered me an innocent victim and therefore someone worthy of her sympathy" (p. 114). Even when the family is relocated to Guguletu and Mandisa is upset about having to go to a school where she knows nobody, her mother **is cold and unsympathetic**, telling her many other children would love to change places with her (pp. 31–32).

Tata

He doesn't play a large role in the novel. Despite the patriarchal nature of the society it describes, men are surprisingly absent in the story. Tata has two brothers, Middle Father and Little Father, as Mandisa calls them, who are involved in the negotiations surrounding her child and marriage with China (see p. 124).

Mandisa's father

Tata is a **kind and gentle man** who is more sympathetic to Mandisa's needs and wishes (pp. 128–131) than her mother, but he eventually gives in to tradition and social pressure and tells her she must marry China.

Khaya

He is one year older than Mandisa (p. 96). Like Mandisa, he is a good student (p. 31). He eventually marries and starts a family with Mandisa's best friend Nono.

Mandisa's brother

Nono

Mandisa's best friend as a teenager, until she discovered that Nono had been secretly involved with Mandisa's brother (p. 89). They mend their friendship. Nono and Khaya have a daughter together. It is the news of Nono's pregnancy which alarms Mandisa's mother so much that she decides to send her daughter away from the township to live with her grandparents in their ancestral village of Gungululu.

Later Khaya's wife

3.4   Characters

Nobulumku – Khaya and Nono's daughter

Funiwe

Mandisa's aunt

(Makhulu's younger daughter – see pp. 102, 109–114). Funiwe is a wilder personality than her sister, Mandisa's mother. She writes to Makhulu that she will be returning to the ancestral village of Gungululu because she is expecting a child. Makhulu is surprised but delighted by the news.

Warm and relaxed

Funiwe is a tough and large personality. She is the first to notice that Mandisa is pregnant, and once the confusion has been cleared up, she defends the girl against her mother, arguing that as the pregnancy was an unfortunate accident, Mandisa has not brought shame on her family. Funiwe is much warmer and more relaxed than her sister, Mandisa's mother. She argues: "We must support and protect [Mandisa] now." (p. 113)

Malume – Mandisa's uncle (p. 102).

Makhulu

Mandisa's grand-mother

She (introduced on p. 93) is a kindly old woman who takes care of Mandisa in 1972 when Mandisa's mother banishes her from the township. Mandisa learns that she is pregnant with Mxolisi while she is in Gungululu with Makhulu and Funiwe (Mandisa is 15 at the time).

Makhulu is patient and caring: "[she] helped keep me not only sane … but bodily alive" (p. 100). She makes efforts to learn what food Mandisa likes and to cook for her. Her kindness and gentle nature are contrasted sharply with Mandisa's mother's coldness and what Mandisa sees as her mother's rejection of her (see p. 101). Makhulu is illiterate (see Mandisa's comments when she asks to see

3.4 Characters

the letter from Funiwe, pp. 102–103) and has, it can be assumed, never left the village in which she lives.

Tatomkhulu – Mandisa's grandfather (p. 173–183). The father of Tata teaches Mandisa about the history, prophecies and legends of the Xhosa, correcting the things she learns in school.

China's family

Mandisa does not have a good relationship with China's family during the brief but important period in which she learns that she is pregnant, they get married and live together for two years before he runs away. China's family tries to make her feel unwelcome: A traditional initiation period for a new wife is filled with humiliations and insults (p. 140). They give her mocking ritual names and when China runs away she is blamed for not having been able to keep him, for having done something wrong and been a bad wife (pp. 131–145). China's father is so upset about his son running away that he stops coming to visit Tooksie, his niece (with whose aunt Mandisa and China had been living with their baby – p. 133), and also stops giving them money. Mandisa has to get a job and finds herself working even harder. Unable to work, care for her baby and continue to do the traditional chores of a makoti, she leaves China's family and finds a room of her own (p. 145).

Father, mother, aunt

Friends and neighbours

Mzamo and Zazi – Mxolisi's boyhood friends, sons of a woman in whose garden hokkie Mandisa and Mxolisi live. The two boys are older than Mxolisi but enjoy playing with him. They were hiding and Mxolisi, thinking it was a game, betrayed their hiding place. After this Mxolisi stops talking for almost two years (see pp. 146–148).

Shot by the police

3.4   Characters

Vuyo and Sis' Lulu – Mandisa's childhood friend and her mother in Guguletu. Their family is forcibly separated during the resettlements from their previous home to the new-built township of Guguletu. Mandisa hears later that Lulu and one of her twins has died (pp. 92–93)

Stella – a childhood friend of Mandisa's from Blouvlei whom she coincidentally meets again in Guguletu (pp. 89–93). She is 14 at the time and they encounter one another in the white district of Claremont. She is much more worldly than Mandisa – she smokes, wears a bra, gossips about their old friends – and she seems to have an intense and frightening capacity for hatred in her which alarms Mandisa.

Sazi (Mxolisi's lieutenant) and **Lwazi** (a follower of Mxolisi), both mentioned on p. 16. They serve no function in the plot but illustrate the respect and status Mxolisi has within the youth movement in Guguletu. Another young man in the group is **Lumko**, a friend of Mxolisi's "in the bush" (p. 18, suggesting that they had undergone their coming of age rituals together).

Ribba – classmate of Mandisa's who dies having an illegal abortion in 1973 (p. 95).

Skonana

Mandisa's neighbour

Skonana is an older single woman without children. She is a gossip and a "Shebeen Queen" (p. 46) – meaning she is a popular and important figure in the gossip-driven gatherings at shebeens (places where cheap alcohol is produced). She is nosy and intrusive, enjoys drama and she seems to take a kind of sadistic pleasure in sharing bad news. It seems clear that Mandisa and Dwadwa only tolerate

3.4   Characters

her because they have to live next to one another. Skonana later comes to visit Mandisa together with other neighbours in order to offer comfort and support, embodying the positive aspects of the community and putting her own interests aside for the time being.

Qwati – Another neighbour (p. 166+). Qwati is in her early 60s and has problems with varicose veins in her legs. She is very friendly, and is diabetic, asthmatic and probably an alcoholic too.

Other characters

The other mother

This character is **invisible and silent**. Mandisa is telling her the story of the book, and therefore of her own life: the mother of the white girl murdered by Mxolisi is the blank page receiving Mandisa's story. We know nothing about her. She is a presence throughout the book, as we are encouraged by the story itself to imagine her pain and grief as we learn more about Mandisa's pain and grief. We are constantly reminded, by the juxtaposition of passages about the white girl and Mxolisi, of the extremes of human nature and attitudes to life, and of **the great loss suffered by both mothers**. The mother of the dead white girl is like Mandisa's shadow within the novel: It says nothing and does nothing, but helps us, the readers, to see the outlines of Mandisa's life and character.

Mother of the
white girl

The dead white girl

> "Such a kind heart, this friend from overseas." (p. 11)

The white girl (based on Amy Biehl) is a sunny-natured, kind-hearted person, full of optimism and a desire to help others. She is unaware

Amy Biehl
(1967–1993)

3.4 Characters

of the danger she places herself in when she drives her friends home to Guguletu; having only good thoughts in her own heart and mind, she seems to be incapable of believing in the darkness and hatred in others. She is killed by Mxolisi after she is spotted by a mob of angry protesters.

For further information on the real Amy Biehl, see chapter 5 – Materials (p. 130).

Other secondary characters

Mandisa's employer

Mrs Nelson is the white woman Mandisi ("Mandy") works for. She is introduced on p. 20. The strongest impression we get of Mrs Nelson is that she is a fearful woman: She is afraid of getting old, afraid of getting fat, and she is terrified of any kind of trouble involving the blacks. When she hears that there is trouble in Guguletu she is in a panic to get rid of Mandisa.

Mrs Nelson has children, a husband, and a widowed friend (wife of a white officer who had fought in the Boer Wars, apparently) called Mrs Joan. **She doesn't work, does nothing around the house**, but needs a "day off" to rest every week. Mandisa is astonished by the woman's weakness and laziness, and she gives no sign that she has any respect for Mrs Nelson when she mentions her.

Tat'uNonjayikhali is a worker and a friend of Mandisa's family in Blouvlei. He appears in Mandisa's happy recollections of her childhood in Blouvlei and he represents in the novel **the togetherness and warmth of an intact community**. He is very generous (pp. 51–52) and thought of as unreliable (p. 53) because he has neither a wife nor children.

3.4 Characters

Manono is much less strict than Mandisa's mother; she lets Nono wear what clothes she likes and doesn't seem to worry so much about boys and sex (p. 95). When she learns that Mandisa's mother has begun insulting Nono because of her relationship with Khaya, she stands up for her daughter and confronts the other woman directly (pp. 96–97).

Nono's mother

Reverend (Mfundisi) Mananga – a priest, from the Anglican church of St Mary Magdalene in Guguletu. He works with Mxolisi and the other groups of black youths in the township. He is involved with the activist group to which Mxolisi belongs and is part of the network trying to hide and protect the young man following the killing of the white girl (see p. 186). We see him on the morning of that day as well: Mxolisi and the other young men come to his church looking for space to hold a meeting, but there is none available. The priest whispers to Mxolisi (p. 13) when the crowd starts getting restless and angry, and Mxolisi leads them away. This brief moment suggests two things: that the priest is sympathetic and somehow involved in the protest movement, and that **Mxolisi has considerable influence** as a leader among the youths.

Involved in the protest movement

Constellations

Mandisa and Mxolisi are at the centre of the novel. Everything moves around these two figures – Mxolisi is the focus of the story, being the killer of the white girl, and Mandisa is the storyteller. The white girl is an almost accidental presence, having no direct relationship to any of the characters.

Main characters: Mandisa and Mxolisi

This book is essentially **the story of Mandisa's life**, and so the clearest way to organise the characters in *Mother to Mother* in order to help you get an overview of their relationships and connections is in the form of a classic family tree, showing the generations of

3.4 Characters

Mandisa's family within the clan. All other characters are connected from their positions outside this family structure.

Family tree (see graphic p. 83)

(grandparents)
→ Makhulu – maternal grandmother
→ Tatomkhulu – paternal grandfather

(Parents' generation)
→ 'Mama'– Mandisa's mother
→ Funiwe – sister of Mama
→ Malume – brother of Mama
→ Tata – Mandisa's father
→ Middle Father, Little Father – brothers of Tata

(Mandisa's generation)
→ Mandisa and Khaya (brother of Mandisa)
→ Mandisa's husbands China, Lungile and Dwadwa

(children's generation)
→ Mxolisi
→ Lunga
→ Siziwe

[All other characters]

3.4 Characters

MANDISA'S FAMILY TREE

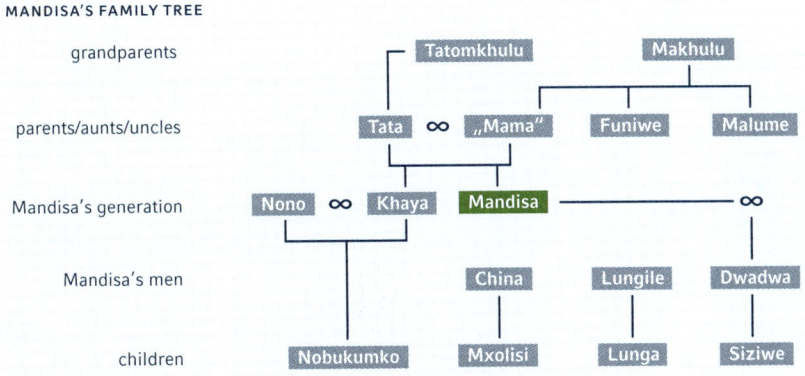

grandparents	Tatomkhulu	Makhulu
parents/aunts/uncles	Tata ∞ „Mama"	Funiwe	Malume
Mandisa's generation	Nono ∞ Khaya	Mandisa ∞
Mandisa's men	China	Lungile	Dwadwa
children	Nobukumko	Mxolisi	Lunga	Siziwe

3.5 Themes

The primary, interconnected themes of *Mother to Mother* we will look at here are issues of
- → identity and inequality (most importantly when it comes to race and gender)
- → violence and oppression
- → positive and negative aspects of communities, families and traditions
- → grief, guilt, hope and despair.

These themes are all important within the larger narrative theme of an investigation of the past – what happened (the murder of the white girl) and why (the environment which produced Mxolisi)? This theme is a structural device which defines the form of the narrative. It is at the root of all the themes the novel tackles, and goes further back, beyond Mandisa's own story, to the history of white settlers in South Africa and the fundamental crime of colonialism, which led to the apartheid state.

IDENTITY & INEQUALITY –
Who am I, and who am I allowed to be?

Racial identity

The apartheid state in South Africa was explicitly **organised around identity** – specifically racial identity. And as we see in Mandisa's recollections of her own life, her culture (the Xhosa clan) also has a great deal to say about identity, in this case, specifically **gender identity** – the duties and responsibilities of a daughter, wife and mother, and the limited freedoms of women in a strictly patriarchal culture.

3.5 Themes

These two issues of **racial and gender identity** are inescapable themes in Sindiwe Magona's novel, and they are the base upon which everything else rests – the plot, the characters, and the world surrounding the narrator.

TEXT	REFERENCE (PP.)	NOTES
White people stole our land.	173	The most direct expression possible of the truth of European-South African history, this accusation is repeated a couple of times in the novel. It is the unavoidable and un-ambiguous foundation upon which everything in South Africa is built. The injustice of the society, the disruption in the history of the tribes, the crippling of entire generations, the brutalisation of communities and the levels of distrust and hatred between the races which will take many, many years to heal: All of this, and everything Sindiwe Magona is talking about in Mother to Mother, comes back to this simple truth.
Stole them from us. STOLE everything from us.	116	The taxi driver who brings Mandisa and her mother back to Guguletu from Gungululu is astonished at the size of the herds of cattle owned by one white farmer, and becomes increasingly angry at the way the white settlers had stolen everything from the original people of the country.

3.5 Themes

TEXT	REFERENCE (PP.)	NOTES
"[…] the biggest storm is still here. It is in our hearts […] deep run the roots of hatred here."	175	Mandisa is taught by her grandfather about the history and legends of the Xhosa. He teaches her about the coming of the white people and how the country was stolen from the native inhabitants. The storm he refers to is the hatred the black South Africans feel for the white colonisers, and for the brutal racist oppression they imposed on a country which had, until their arrival, been free. This conversation is very important, both for Mandisa's understanding of her tribe and her community's history, and also for us as readers: Mandisa's final thoughts on how and why her son killed the white girl have to do with this idea of hatred as a something rooted in the past and growing out into the present and the future.
His father went to the Police Station. Then, to the hospitals. Phoned each and every one of those that had wards for black people.	144	Not all hospitals in South Africa would accept black patients: this startling example of the concrete effects of the apartheid system is thrown out casually at the end of a sentence.
We were avoiding the main roads […] because of fear of harassment from the Traffic Cops, 'Who will stop a car driven by a black man as a matter of course.'	115	On the way back from Gungululu to Guguletu, the taxi driver knows from experience that black drivers will be automatically stopped by the police and takes a much longer, roundabout route. This is another example of how institutionalised, everyday racist behaviour can have concrete, negative effects on black South Africans' lives.

3.5 Themes

TEXT	REFERENCE (PP.)	NOTES
That is what the white woman I work for calls me: Mandy. [...] Says she can't say any of our native names because of the clicks. My name is Mandisa. MA-NDI-SA. Do you see any click in that?	20	Here is an example of the petty and constant racism of a segregated society. Mrs Nelson refuses to call Mandisa by her real name, giving her instead a kind of pet name. This is humiliating and patronising: It puts Mandisa on the level of a child or an animal, and indicates that Mrs Nelson doesn't see her or want to treat her as an adult woman and an individual worthy of respect.
Fear. Shame. Anger. My whole world had simply collapsed and was no more. I shrunk; because he was.	113 114 142	An unwanted teenage pregnancy, an unmarried girl: Mandisa's initial reactions to learning that she is pregnant are overwhelmingly negative. She sees that in the society in which she lives she will lose everything – not just the opportunities she wanted to study, to make a better life for herself as a black person in a white-dominated, racist society, but also the rejection and humiliation she will experience in a community in which women are subject to very strict expectations.
How could it possibly be my fault that China had taken himself wherever it was he had gone? But his father was not quite done with me. [...] "I leave you here with my son," he said. "And now, I find him gone. He is not here. But you are still here, with your son [...]."	143	Mandisa feels that China's family, in particular his father, blame her for China having left. In a patriarchal society like this, the women are subject to much stricter rules governing their behaviour. The situation is common: When things go wrong, the women are the first to be blamed.

3.5   Themes

TEXT	REFERENCE (PP.)	NOTES
"Try to give him more breast than bottle," said my husband, reminding me his father gave him but so much a week.	142	Here is another example of how a patriarchal society enables men to interfere in the lives of women. China, being lazy and untrustworthy, is not earning much money. His father gives him some. But he doesn't like having to spend the money on bottled milk, and so instructs his wife to breastfeed more.
Khaya, because he was a boy, didn't suffer from restrictions as I did.	56	Here is a series of examples from the book of gender inequality.
"Nono should have taken better care of herself [...]. It is the girl's responsibility, as far as I'm concerned [...]." Instead of blaming Khaya, Mama said, "Manono should look in the mirror and ask herself what it was she had failed to do for such a thing to happen to her daughter." [...] Khaya, she pointed out, could not be blamed.	97	1 & 2 Khaya is Mandisa's brother. He has more freedom as a child because he is a boy. When Mandisa becomes pregnant, her mother has a total meltdown, but Khaya is not to be blamed when he gets his girlfriend pregnant.
Instead, I was forced into being a wife, forever abandoning my dreams, hopes, aspirations. For ever.	133	3 & 4 The role of wife is one of subservience to the husband's family. She must endure a period of "training" (the ukuhota) during which she works like a slave and is ordered around by everyone in the family. China is not expected to do more than he did before.
[Mandisa describes how much work she does every day during her ukuhota]	140	

3.5 Themes

TEXT	REFERENCE (PP.)	NOTES
[...] how to approach this man, who wielded so much power over my little life?	142	5 As China's father and the head of the household, Mandisa's father in law has full authority over her. As a young woman she has no voice in the household.
Your daughter. The imperfect atonement of her race. My son. The perfect host of the demons of his. [...]	201–210	Towards the end of the novel we find three very significant sets of short, paired statements about the white girl and Mxolisi. They are poetic, dense expressions of the symbolic importance of the two characters and what they represent in the context of South Africa and the catastrophe of racial hatred which has defined the history of the country. 1 (p. 201) These two lines are extremely significant. The dead girl and Mxolisi are taken here by Mandisa as being symbolic of the identity of their respective races. As a white person, the girl is an "imperfect atonement" – atonement the act of showing that you are sorry for a wrong that has been done in the past, here specifically the crimes of colonialism and apartheid. As a black man, Mxolisi is the "perfect host of the demons" of the black race. In this case the demons are parasites and Mxolisi is the host in which these demons live. The demons are the hatred Mandisa's grandfather told her about, and the violence Mandisa knows

3.5   Themes

TEXT	REFERENCE (PP.)	NOTES
		was encouraged and tolerated among the youths by the adults who should have known better. There is a sad irony in the contrast of the words here: the "Imperfect" life and behaviour of the white girl, who had been a good, helpful, compassionate person, and Mxolisi the "perfect host", who is a vessel for violence, hatred and death.
One boy. Lost. Hope-lessly lost. One girl, far away from home. [...]		2 (p. 210) A few pages later, at the very end of the novel, we have another de-ceptively simple pair of statements about the girl and Mxolisi. Mxolisi is at home, where he was raised and where his people are, but he is figuratively speaking lost, without support or guidance or roots. The corrupting nature of the racism of South African society has left him without any way to orientate himself, as it has with millions of other young people. And the girl is in a place she should not have been, as Mandisa repeatedly says: Why was she there? Was there nowhere in her world she could have helped and done good deeds? Why did she have to come to a world in which she was an alien, where she was not welcome, a world she didn't understand well enough to be able to survive?

3.5   Themes

TEXT	REFERENCE (PP.)	NOTES
My son, the blind but sharpened arrow of the wrath of his race. Your daughter, the sacrifice of hers. Blindly chosen. Flung towards her sad fate by fortune's cruellest slings.		3 (p. 210) At the very end the symbolism is more violent and cruel. Mxolisi is characterised as a weapon and the girl is explicitly called a "sacrifice". The conflict is not resolved and there is no "happy end": Mxolisi is described as the weaponised hatred of the oppressed black people of South Africa, and the girl as the random, unchosen sacrifice of the whites, a useless expression of guilt.
[Mxolisi] had already seen his tomorrows; in the defeated stoop of his father's shoulders. In the tired eyes of that father's friends. In the huddled, ragged men who daily wait for chance at some job whose whereabouts they do not know … wait at the corners of roads leading nowhere … […] But chance has not come that way today. Chance rarely came that way. Any day. Chance has been busy in that other world … the white world.	203	At the end of the novel, Mandisa talks about the future her son has seen for himself in the world around him. All that he has experienced and seen – the results of the flow of time to where he stands – has shown him that he has no future. There is nothing ahead for him but poverty and powerlessness.

3.5 Themes

TEXT	REFERENCE (PP.)	NOTES
My son was only an agent, executing the long-simmering dark desires of his race. Burning hatred for the oppressor possessed his being. It saw through his eyes; walked with his feet and wielded the knife that tore mercilessly into her flesh. The resentment of three hundred years plugged his ears; deaf to her pitiful entreaties.	210	These are Mandisa's last thoughts in the novel on the role her son has played. In keeping with the underlying concept of individuals being just small factors in an ever-flowing continuum of life and time, he becomes here a symbol, an agent into which the accumulated centuries of hatred and oppression have flowed and through which they find expression. The hatred Mandisa's grandfather talks about (see above) is characterised as having roots, and Mandisa is talking of it as an active, personified force, like a demon which has taken possession of her son.

VIOLENCE, HATRED & DEHUMANISATION:
The police and the Young Lions

Historical roots

The violence and oppression in the novel are very much the products of the racist society created in South Africa following the colonisation by white Europeans. The oppression has historical roots, and became over time more and more **a part of society**, defined by law and enforced by a brutal and merciless state. Violence goes back and forth in the novel, and we see not only examples of brutal behaviour by white police against black South Africans, but also of course the violence of black protestors against a white girl and the violence of blacks against blacks (most horribly seen in the "necklacing" of suspected counter-revolutionary traitors; p. 77).

How could it happen?

Because Sindiwe Magona is trying in her novel to illustrate how environment and history made the Amy Biehl murder possible, as

3.5 Themes

she says in her Author's Preface, we can see that she understands the violence and brutality to be the **products and the consequences of a system of injustice and oppression**. Black South Africans have been made more brutal by their environment and their experiences, she argues. Generations have experienced racially-motivated oppression which has broken up communities and critically affected individuals' ability to move around, to earn money and to live freely. This experience of oppression contributes to a growing sense of **frustration, depression, anger, hatred and despair** – strong and negative feelings which can find no healthy expression because the people are so helpless and demoralised by their oppression. As community bonds are weakened and individuals are turned against one another, **fear and violence replace the values of a healthy society** (this corrupting effect of the brutality of the apartheid state and its effects on the growth of crime in the black townships is strikingly illustrated by Magona's metaphor of maggots growing in warm, wet earth – see below for the relevant quotation).

We see other examples of violence in the novel. Mxolisi is so traumatised by seeing policemen shoot two friends of his that he stops talking for two years. Mandisa's house is raided at night by abusive police officers. When the slums are cleared in her childhood she sees police and military working together to literally destroy the homes of her people. Violence and brutal behaviour are present throughout Mandisa's life and even in 1993, at the supposed end of the apartheid state, the cycles of violence, oppression and despair continue.

Violence against blacks

3.5 Themes

TEXT	REFERENCE (PP.)	NOTES
The police are not our friends.	44	This blunt statement is reinforced by incidents throughout Mandisa's story. The police never help or provide support or protection. They are viewed exclusively as a dangerous extension of an oppressive and unjust system.
Guguletu is a violent place. Every day one hears of someone who was killed…	44	Mandisa here sets the scene for the reader, after having just heard from her white employer, Mrs Nelson, that there is trouble in the township. This again is a very clear statement about the conditions in which she and her family and neighbours must live.
[The police are] an affliction. We know that many innocent people have died in their hands. [...] Killed by the police. With impunity they killed our people in the past. Therefore the perpetrators of evil, those who have made crime a career, live in the benign atmosphere cultivated by that corruption. As warm wet dirt breeds maggots … so have criminals thrived. Sheltered by the police who conducted deeds even worse than theirs. [...] Violence is rife. It has become a way of life.	44–45	This key passage is a little more complex than the statements mentioned above. Mandisa's point here is that the widespread brutality and everyday violence of the police – the authorities – help to create an environment in which violence and brutality can flourish and grow. The experience of so many blacks in South Africa is that violence is a part of life, and instead of trying to find another way to live, they become a part of the systems of brutality and violence. The metaphor Mandisa uses here describes the kind of environment in which maggots can grow, reinforcing her point that it is the authorities (police), the system (apartheid) and the adults (as with the violence of the Young Lions: see below for more) which are to blame for creating an environment in which the "corruption" of brutality can grow and spread.

3.5 Themes

TEXT	REFERENCE (PP.)	NOTES
Mandisa describes the evolution of the youth protest movements from politically-minded activism aimed at the apartheid state, in particular the terrible state of education for blacks, to the rise of black-on-black violent crime and racial attacks driven by hatred of whites. This passage is about the Young Lions, as the youth protestors were called, and Mandisa's horror as the violence began to turn against other blacks, culminating in the horrible practice of "necklacing" suspected informers and traitors. The practice of necklacing is even compared to the guillotine, which was used to execute counter-revolutionaries in the French Revolution (1789–1799).	73–77	In this passage, Mandisa tries to explain how the student/youth protests developed over time from vandalism to murder, from protests against (white) power structures to the barbaric murders of (black) counter-revolutionaries. Her main point is that it is the generation of parents and leaders and teachers who are to blame for the increasingly unrestrained and immoral levels of violence and brutality on the part of the black youth. She sees the adults as being guilty for the crimes of the young. This is consistent with the book's treatment of events and individuals as being products of a continuously moving flow of events: Nothing happens without a cause or a point of origin, nothing happens in a vacuum, and in this case, she is saying that the older generation is partially responsible for the atrocities committed by the younger. Another point in this important passage is that the narrator is obviously upset by the evolution of the protests, from political activism protesting injustice and specific topics like inadequate education, to a wave of racially-charged ("Whites are dogs!") violence which is powered more by hatred than by a desire to try to change things for the better. The sheer negativity and nihilism of this violence is frightening to most people.

3.5 Themes

TEXT	REFERENCE (PP.)	NOTES
An army of policemen [...]. (p. 84) The voice is raised and angry. It is a hideous voice [...]. There is something not human about it. (p. 85) They practically pulled the house apart [...]. They pulled the floor boards up. They knocked a wall down. (p. 86) [...] hey beat up Lunga [...] (p. 87) Nothing would ever be the same for us. (p. 87)	79–87	A large group of policemen raid Mandisa's house in the night looking for Mxolisi. They destroy much of the house, tear the boys' hokkie to pieces, slap Mandisa and beat up her son Lunga. The very rough treatment seems to be out of all proportion, in particular when considering that the boy they're seeking, Mxolisi, isn't even present. But as Mandisa had feared when her neighbour told her what had happened, the killing of a white girl (and American as well) is a whole new level of trouble for the people in the township, a crime the white authorities have to deal with as quickly and powerfully as possible. There is little in this passage to interpret or analyse; it is a fairly straightforward account of the distress and chaos of a quick and brutal raid by police at night. As an event, it is important in the story, and as an explicit description of the brutality of South African life it is a prime example of the theme of violence in the novel.

3.5 Themes

TEXT	REFERENCE (PP.)	NOTES
[...] the police stormed into the house. (p. 147) "Where are the boys [...]?" (p. 147) "Here they are, in the wardrobe!" screamed Mxolisi, pointing to the wardrobe. A clever little smile all over his chubby face. He said those terrible words and, swift as a wink, witnessed their outcome. The boys jumped out and made for the window. But when they hit the back garden the police were waiting, and shot them then and there. He was struck mute by what he saw the police do to the two boys. (p. 148) [...] – for the next two years. (p. 148)	146–148	Mxolisi's friends are involved in the student boycotts and are being hunted by the police. Mxolisi is a little boy, thinks it's a game of hide and seek, and betrays them: The police shoot them when they try to escape. The guilt and trauma Mxolisi feels never leaves him (see p. 158). The impact of witnessing the killing is one thing, but his role in it makes it even worse. This encounter with violence and death changes everything for Mxolisi as much as Mandisa's pregnancy at the age of 15 changed everything for her.

3.5 Themes

TEXT	REFERENCE (PP.)	NOTES
[*Mxolisi is known in the neighbourhood for having rescued a girl from being raped*] "This boy of yours has a good heart, " [...]. (p. 162) "There were many people there. [...] None stopped the crime, none. Until your son arrived on the scene."	162–163	Mxolisi doesn't only embody violence and hatred. He is also known to be a good young man, with a sense of right and wrong and the courage to defend the weak.
And these days, something is always happening in Guguletu. Or in Langa. Or Nyanga. Since the schoolchildren started boycotting classes, way back in '76, when the riots in Soweto came down to Cape Town. [...] Haven't we lived with these children's riots since '76? [...] These tyrants our children have become, power crazed [...]. I, for one, have had it up to here, with all this nonsense.	23–25	Mandisa is talking here about the student protests which began in the 1970s and continued up to and past the end of the apartheid regime. She is annoyed by the student protests and the constant demands from the younger generation. She talks later on in greater detail about the violence and how it became worse over time, but this sets the scene: There has been widespread unrest and protests, children have been boycotting school – meaning that they have been getting no education and spending all their time out on the streets. At this point in her story, Mandisa has no idea that her son Mxolisi is involved in the trouble. All she knows is what her white employer told her: that something has happened in Guguletu.

3.5 Themes

TEXT	REFERENCE (PP.)	NOTES
[Forced resettlement and inadequate housing in Guguletu]	27–34	Not all violence involves individuals causing physical harm to one another. In this passage from Mandisa's memories of her family being forcibly moved to the township from their home in Blouvlei, we see a detailed and personal account of institutional violence: the state tells the people where to go, destroying their homes to make sure they leave, and forces them to live in a bad place which breaks up their communities and leads to a growth in poverty, crime and discontent. The blacks are treated as being less than human by the apartheid regime, and are shuffled around like cattle.
[The killing of the white girl by the mob]	204–209	The last chapter in the novel describes how the white girl is spotted and killed by the angry mob in Guguletu. The shocking brutality of the scene shows how the mob, themselves dehumanised in their lust for blood, refuse (or are unable) to recognise the girl as a human being, seeing in her instead just a symbol of the hated white oppressors who have made their lives a living hell for generations.
[For many years] we have lived with violence. This was nothing new to us. What was new was that this time, the victim was white. A white person killed in Guguletu, a black township.	69	Not all violence is equal. Everyone understands that black people killing other black people is nowhere near as serious as black people killing white people. The implication is clear that the death of a white girl in a black township will lead to a whole new level of trouble for the township.

3.5 Themes

TEXT	REFERENCE (PP.)	NOTES
The attacks on the Belgian nuns in 1960	70	Mandisa recalls an incident involving white nuns who had heard of the atrocities being committed against the blacks and had come to South Africa to help. They were beaten by a group of black men. This is another example of the senseless violence which is repeated in the killing of the white girl in 1993, and foreshadowed by the self-destructive acts of the cattle killing movement in the 19th century. While each of these incidents is different, they share at heart a tendency towards a type of violence which is fuelled by a mixture of helplessness, hatred and ignorance.
"Make the country ungovernable!"	73	This command from activist leaders to the youth movements and student protestors is a clear call for insurrection and extreme protest.

COMMUNITY, FAMILY, TRADITION & HISTORY –
Strength and support/oppression and limitation

Ambivalent

Traditions, communities and families, customs and rituals – these issues are treated with a degree of ambivalence in the novel. In the rural village of Gungululu and in the rites surrounding her marriage to China and the birth of her son, the young Mandisa experiences them sometimes as a **source of support and identity**, but mostly as a **restrictive, oppressive limit** on her feelings and ideas about her own future and dreams. The older Mandisa is pained by the breakdown of traditional customs and communities, because she sees that without them, her people are becoming lost.

3.5   Themes

The messages of **Xhosa tribal legends** are equally ambivalent – the story of the doomed, suicidal cattle killing movement, for example, shows a frustrating mixture of dignity, rebellion, strength and superstitious stupidity (pp. 177–179).

The overwhelming impression of the role of traditional communities and customs – including an understanding of one's own roots back through time, through generations to a mythical past – is that these are **imperfect but important structures** which can provide strength, comfort and identity to keep individuals rooted and to provide them with the confidence that comes with a sense of who you are, where you come from and where you belong. The restrictions and frustrations which come with a certain **lack of freedom of choice** – especially for women and girls – are an aspect which reflects the complexity of life and the ambivalence at the heart of Mandisa's narrative: Nothing is simple.

Where you belong

The location of Gungululu in the novel is very important when it comes to this group of themes (Mandisa's time in the village is described on pp. 99–114). Mandisa's mother sends her back to the ancestral village to protect her from the immoral influences of the township; she sees the old rural village as being a purer **place of strong traditions and healthy tribal and family values.**

Gugululu

The theme of community is of course very closely interconnected with the theme of identity.

3.5 Themes

TEXT	REFERENCE (PP.)	NOTES
There is knowledge with which I was born [...].	173	This statement made at the opening of chapter 10 is an important comment by Mandisa on the issues of identity and community and tradition. She positions herself within the history of her tribe and people: Each new generation receives the knowledge and wisdom of the generations which came before. What this continuity of knowledge and identity means in practical terms is that the communities within the tribal structures have a coherent and inclusive sense of identity. Mandisa knows what her place is in the world; she feels that she is part of something larger than any individual.
China, too, needed to change his status. No boy can take a wife. He had to go and get himself circumcised. (p. 126) The importance of customs (pp. 128–131) "Unfortunately, daughter [...] we are ruled by laws. We live our lives through advice, consultation and allowing or bowing down to the voice of the majority. Never can I trust my eye above the eyes of the many, who are my family, my clan." (p. 128)	124–140	In this section of chapter 8 we see many examples of tribal customs, rituals and traditions. – In order to marry, China must become a man, and the rite of passage from boyhood to manhood is for the Xhosa the ritual of circumcision, performed out in the bush by tribal elders. – Mandisa's father tells her that she must marry China, society demands it. He expresses here the concept of a tribal community being in its entirety more powerful and more important than any individual, individuals have to adapt and conform to what the majority thinks is right.

3.5 Themes

TEXT	REFERENCE (PP.)	NOTES
Custom dictated that he listened to the counsel of the clan. (p. 131) Naming conventions (see p. 134) [...] I knew the ritual. Someone would bring me a cup of tea and call out a name. I could refuse the tea till a name I liked came up. On the other hand, if my in-laws wanted to be nasty, they could stop at some point and give me no alternative. [...] It was the custom to leave all the things of one's girlhood behind, including the name. (S. 134–135) Marriage negotiations (p. 136) *ukuhota* (initiation of the wife) p. 140		– Mandisa's baby has to be named, and this is not something she is allowed, by custom, to do herself, the husband's family must be involved. She also is supposed to lose her own name upon becoming a wife. – The rituals before and after the wedding are complex and, for Mandisa, extremely annoying. The two families argue constantly about money and who has to do what. Once she is married she enters an initiation period in which she is treated very badly by her new family. She is worked harder than any servant and is still expected to perform as a model mother. The reader shouldn't forget that Mandisa is at this point still a young girl, only 15 years old.

3.5 Themes

TEXT	REFERENCE (PP.)	NOTES
China's father [...] came up with the idea we take Mxolisi to see a *sangoma*. [...] I was desperate enough to try anything. (p. 152–153)	152–156	China's father suggests that Mandisa should take Mxolisi to see a sangoma – a faith healer – because he has stopped talking and the doctors can't help him. The woman is angry at Mandisa but pities her. She tells Mandisa that she must "free" her son, that children are sensitive and know when they are hated – but she then changes her mind and says that resentment is a more appropriate word than hate. She sees that Mxolisi carries a terrible burden for such a young child, and she sees how much Mandisa resents her own son. Mandisa takes the words of the sangoma seriously. She can't lie to herself: She knows that she has a complicated relationship with her son and that she has very ambivalent feelings towards him.
Gungululu is the village where Mama's family comes from. It is a place: 'where children still know how to behave' (p. 99) [...] where children were named according to the spaces between the years of rain. (p. 99)	99	Mandisa is sent to the village when she is nearly 14. Her mother wants to protect her from the moral dangers of the crowded, chaotic township. The village seems to exist in another time; life there is slower and more closely bound to traditions and older, tribal customs.

3.5 Themes

TEXT	REFERENCE (PP.)	NOTES
That was part of the problem: this throwing together of so many, many people, all at once, into a new place. (p. 28) [...] where before we had been members of solid, well-knit communities, now we were among strangers [...]. (p. 29) We die young, these days. In the times of our grandmothers and their grandmothers before them, African people lived to see their great-great-grandchildren. Today, one is lucky to see a grandchild. (p. 32) Guguletu killed us ... killed the thing that held us together ... made us human. [...] for some reason, the small, inadequate, ugly concrete houses seemed to loosen ties among those who dwelled in them. (p. 33–34)	28–34	Mandisa talks about the lasting effects of the forced resettlements into the new townships. Communities are broken, families torn apart, and bonds and connections which have existed for generations are broken. The resulting depression and fragmentation has very real consequences. Poverty increases, families fall apart, crime rates rise at increasingly alarming levels, people die younger. What Mandisa sees in Gungululu is a memory of what life may once have been like, with a simpler, cleaner, more peaceful and more community-based life.

3.5 Themes

TEXT	REFERENCE (PP.)	NOTES
In time we did not remember coming back from school to mothers waiting with smiles.	67	The move to Guguletu changes everything for the former residents of Blouvlei. Mandisa finds many ways to express how traumatic and damaging the relocation was, but this final comment is striking in its poignant expression of a child's perspective on what has happened: there are no longer happy families. Mothers no longer have time for their children.
"We are people who come to each other's homes when there is a reason," [...]. "We have come to cry with you … as is our custom, to grieve with those who grieve." "We have come to be with you in this time," [...]. It is people such as these who give me strength. And hope.	200–201	Mandisa is surprised in her grief when her neighbours come to her house. This important scene is an expression of the simple, fundamental purpose of a community – to provide mutual support – and it is also a deeply felt reminder of the power of life and love: that despite the violence and poverty and abuse, there is hope, and people can and will help one another through difficult situations.
The afterbirths of our children are deep in this ground.	55	Here is a very vivid image of what "home" can mean to a traditionally organised, tribal community.

3.5 Themes

TEXT	REFERENCE (PP.)	NOTES
Compare and contrast: childhood, growing up, playing, being a child within a community – Mandisa's memories (pp. 49+) versus her children in Guguletu		
[...] I'm supposed to have authority over my children [...].	8	A mother's traditional role is no longer possible in a place in which the mothers have to leave their homes all day in order to work to support their families.
Mandisa's grandfather's stories of colonialism and the cattle killing, the tribe's history	173–183	Mandisa learns a lot from her grandfather about the history of the country before the white people came, and he also teaches her many things which balance or correct what she is taught in school. We can see in this section of the book how the education system under apartheid aimed to rewrite black history. He teaches her about the origins of the hatred in the country: the hatred of the white settlers who stole everything and destroyed the life that had existed before. One specific thing he mentions is the prophecy concerning the "button without a hole", meaning money. The corrupting presence of money changed everything, even more lastingly, it is suggested, than the theft of land. For a culture which had never known money and had never experienced the greed and envy it can inspire, this was a catastrophic development.

3.5   Themes

TEXT	REFERENCE (PP.)	NOTES
		These lessons are an invaluable key to understanding who Mxolisi is, that is, the roots of his hatred and violence. As with everything else in Mother to Mother, his actions do not exist in a vacuum, independent of anything else. Everything is caused by something and everything has consequences. The stories Mandisa's grandfather tell her are about the root causes of what happens in August 1993.
Mxolisi and the underground	185–193	At the end of the novel Mandisa is surprised by a visit from the priest and is sent on a secretive, paranoid journey through a community she had known nothing about. This is the community in which Mxolisi has been active, and in which he is a figure of respect: activist resistance to the political and social status quo. The members of this community have hidden Mxolisi after he killed the girl, and they bring Mandisa to him for purely compassionate reasons – the entire episode is dangerous for all concerned.

GUILT, HOPE, DESPAIR & COPING WITH GRIEF –
From individual pain to cultural trauma

These specific emotional issues are central to the novel. Mandisa, mother of the murderer, is addressing the mother of the murdered girl. The complex and painful issues of grief, guilt, despair and hope in this personal, intimate context are reflected in Mandisa's

3.5 Themes

thoughts about her own life and on the history of her country as a whole.

In addition there is the complex and painful push-and-pull relationship Mandisa has with her son Mxolisi. She loves him and resents him, celebrates him and hates him for having destroyed her life; she grieves for what she lost when he was born; she expresses desperation at the unfairness of having become pregnant in such a freak accident, and she feels guilt and grief for what happens in 1993.

TEXT	REFERENCE (PP.)	NOTES
Our parents believed that education would free us from the slavery that was their lot as uneducated labourers.	88	Mandisa and her brother are supposed to do well at school, which they do – and then go on to educate themselves further in order to improve their position, earn more money, and generally speaking have a better life than their parents. Both children want to pursue this goal. Unfortunately Mandisa becomes pregnant with Mxolisi when she is 15 and all hopes of her bettering herself disappear. Even once she is married to China and living with his family, there is no chance for her to go back to school, as the men in China's family don't think it would proper for a young mother.
Look what the children have done! [...] The one who is dead. Poor child. And her parents. I feel for her parents. For the parents of this poor child, killed by our children. My heart sorrows for them. For her mother.	73	At this point Mandisa knows nothing of Mxolisi's involvement. She only knows that a white girl has been killed in Guguletu. She expresses her sympathy for the grief of the girl's parents, and there is also an indication of guilt ("our children").

3.5 Themes

TEXT	REFERENCE (PP.)	NOTES
I swallow my guilt. What would happen if I stayed home doing all the things a mother's supposed to do? We couldn't possibly survive just on what Dwadwa makes…	8	Mandisa's children want her to make them breakfast because they like it when she does: "We miss your hand" says her son Lunga. But she can't; she has to leave to go to work. She feels guilty – despite having no choice in the matter.
[…] Siziwe squatted on the floor […]. Just a deep dull growl, a trembly sigh, filled with blind despair. […] I tried to stem the haunted, tearless cry. […] Such heaviness of heart in that cry. As of one in darkest despair.	167–170	Siziwe is not physically harmed by the police assault on their home, but she is terrified and driven into a state of fear-driven despair by the event. But later, as Mandisa tries to comfort her daughter, she learns that Siziwe saw Mxolisi return to the house and hide something in the hokkie; she knows more than she is telling Mandisa, however, and refuses to say if anyone else was with Mxolisi. Mandisa feels in a way betrayed by her daughter's refusal to confess everything she knows. She feels that her children see her as being separate, on another side – maybe even as an authority figure who cannot be trusted.
Nothing my son does surprises me any more. Not after that first unbelievable shock, his implanting himself inside me; unreasonably and totally destroying the me I was. The me I would have become.	88	This is a part of one of the passages in the book where Mandisa is directly addressing the other mother. She is here once again expressing the despair and resentment she has felt about her son Mxolisi: the unwanted pregnancy which threw her life completely off course, changing, as she says here, not only who she was, but who she could have become. Mandisa is grieving not only for what

3.5   Themes

TEXT	REFERENCE (PP.)	NOTES
		she actually lost – her childhood, youth, freedom – but also for the dreams and ideas she had about her future. She is grieving for her entire life, in effect, which she blames Mxolisi for having destroyed.
[...] grief, sharp as a new razor.	101	Mandisa is upset at the way her mother has begun to treat her – "Mama left".
[...] my bitter banishment, the serrated knife that ceaselessly tore at the tender flesh of my heart [...].	105	Mandisa's wildly melodramatic adolescent feelings are in a turmoil while she is in Gungululu. She is struggling most importantly with her hopeless infatuation with and separation from China, and to a lesser extent with the unhappiness she feels about how her mother rejected her and banished her to the village. The same two concerns are linked and Mandisa expresses her feelings about them again on p. 108.
But then, there is the terrible guilt I feel he carries. [...] Those friends of his early childhood. Poor children. Died like dogs. Shot by the police. Nobody blamed Mxolisi, he was just a baby then.	159	Mandisa describes how Mxolisi, as a young man involved with the Young Lions, never again betrayed someone else. While he never, ever talks about what happened, his mother knows that the event and his guilt have changed him and left its mark on him for the rest of his life.
"D'you realize she is never going to come back? Dead, means forever?"	197	Mandisa is led to Mxolisi's hiding place and she tries to get the truth out of him. He is evasive but she knows: She can see by the fear and resentful anger in him that he is

3.5 Themes

TEXT	REFERENCE (PP.)	NOTES
		guilty. The enormity of what he has done is hard for either of them to entirely comprehend. Mandisa tries to get him to understand the central fact – that the girl is dead and gone, forever.
Mother of the Slain [...]: I have not slept since. Food turns to sawdust in my mouth. All joy has fled my house and my heart bleeds, it sorrows for you [...].	199	The guilt and grief Mandisa feels is not just for herself and her son. Her child is still alive, come what may: the other mother's daughter is dead, through no fault of her own.
It is people such as these who give me strength. And hope. I hear there are churches and other groups working with young people and grownups. Helping. So that violence may stop.	201	The unexpected expression of communal support from Mandisa's neighbours helps her with her grief and guilt. Nothing can change what has happened, but she sees that something good may yet come out of it.
My Sister-Mother, we are bound in this sorrow. [...] let it console you some, you never have to ask yourself: What did I not do for this child? You can carry your head sky high. You have no shame, no reason for shame. Only the loss. [...] Be consoled, for with your loss comes no shame. No deep sense of personal failure. Only glory.	201–202	Mandisa's words of support and encouragement here to the other mother strongly imply that she applies the opposite to herself. She feels shame. She has loss and shame. She feels that she failed her own child. She feels a deep sense of personal failure.

3.5 Themes

THE ORGANISING THEME – An investigation of the past

The novel looks backwards in time. There has been an event – the death of the girl – and the narrator is looking back into the past, both her own and that of her country, to try and understand and explain how the event came to happen. All of the themes addressed in the novel are **related to this investigation of the past**. The specific facts of the event (the violence of the murder, the central importance of race in the crime, and the presence of the girl in a taboo community) are linked to larger issues of the breakdown of communities and families and the history of racist oppression by colonisers of another race.

Event: death of the white girl

Maybe the most important organising idea in *Mother to Mother* is that **nothing happens without a cause and that nothing happens without consequences**. In this context, the theme of looking into the past to try and help make sense of why a thing has happened or why a person is the way they are makes perfect sense.

Of particular importance to this theme is the chapter (pp. 173–183) in which Mandisa remembers her grandfather teaching her about **the stories from Xhosa tribal history**. In addition to teaching her new things, he corrects the biased lessons she receives in school. He makes her understand how deep a community history or a tribal history is, how important it is for identity and a sense of self, and he helps her to understand how everything is connected to that which came before, and that which comes after. This is the final lesson she learns from what Mxolisi does: that **her son is an arrow fired out of history**, as weaponised symbol of hatred with ancient roots.

History of the Xhosa

3.6 Style and Language

SUMMARY

The novel is framed as a direct address from Mandisa to the dead girl's mother, and the style of the narrative reflects this: it is direct, less formal, and very introspective and emotional. Because it is a first person narrative there can be no question of objectivity or reflective distance: Mandisa is speaking what's in her heart and mind. As far as the use of language goes, two important aspects are the use of Xhosa combined with English, and word usage and sentence structures which are occasionally surprising and strange for Western readers of English.

A subjective and emotional narrative voice

Mandisa's voice

The style and language of the novel are both defined by the content. Mandisa's voice, as **the first person narrator**, is sad, hurt, and introspective, as she tries to explain to herself and to the dead girl's mother how it could have come to the murder. She is digging into her own past and into the past of her country to talk about painful and chaotic feelings and events. She is not reporting in a dispassionate way, even when talking about the country's history and political disturbances: she is talking about how she feels about these things, how she experienced them.

Chapter 1: to the girl's mother

This is clear from the opening of the novel. The **first chapter**, which is the direct address to the dead girl's mother – "My son killed your daughter" (p. 1) – is immediately **direct and naked**.

The opening of **the following chapter** is the first of Mandisa's attempts to imagine what the white girl's life was like on the last day she was alive, and this is also written in a very emotional, un-

3.6 Style and Language

restrained style. There is no attempt at maintaining a dry, objective voice when describing these things which are beyond the knowledge and experience of the person telling the story. The second paragraph in particular ("What thoughts filled her mind as she woke! …" p. 5) is a good example of an unusually **lively and emotional narrative voice**. Exclamation marks are very rarely used in literary writing. The Penguin Writer's Manual, for example, encourages writers not to use them: "if used too frequently, they give a piece of writing an overheated and hysterical or slightly bullying tone" (p. 157).[15]

In this instance, and in this novel, these traditional rules or re-commendations for tone and style cannot be too strictly applied. The voice of the novel – Mandisa's voice – is very emotional and con-flicted, **torn between guilt and grief,** and in this opening passage describing the white girl's last morning she is attempting to express the sunny nature of the girl, her apparently limitless optimism and goodness, and the style of the writing reflects and embodies this, being more excited and informal than is traditionally and predomi-nantly used in literary fiction.

Emotional and conflicted

Mandisa is a passionate character with strong feelings and a stub-born, independent personality (see chapter 3.4). It is no surprise then that her storytelling voice should reflect this. We can com-pare this sunny, excited tone in describing the girl on pages 5–6 with the bleak and emotionally brutalised voice on pages 76–78, **describing the violence of the student protest** movement and the horrific practice of necklacing. Between those extremes we have the reflective tone she uses when recalling **her own childhood and youth**, where she can express the frustrations, joys and confusions she felt with a cool distance and an almost bemused adult maturity.

Brutalised tone

Reflective tone

———

15 Manser, M. & Curtis, S., *The Penguin Writer's Manual*, London 2002.

3.6   Style and Language

The tone of the narrative changes as Mandisa reflects on different subjects. It is noticeable that some of her most detailed and closely-focussed descriptions are of the white girl (see for example pp. 5–6), as she tries to imagine what her final day alive was like. She imagines to the smallest detail how the girl woke up, showered, breakfasted and began to get ready for the day, trying to think of all the things she had to take care of before leaving for the US.

This closely-observed detail is important because it suggests that Mandisa, feeling the huge guilt of being the murderer's mother, is forcing herself to come as close as she can to the girl her son murdered as well as to the girl's mother.

Use of Xhosa

South Africa as a multilingual state

South Africa has **throughout its history** been a multilingual state. From 1910 to 1925 the official languages were Dutch and English, and Afrikaans essentially replaced Dutch from 1925 on. No African languages – with the exception of the Dutch-rooted Afrikaans – were officially recognised until after the end of Apartheid. From 1984 until the end of Apartheid only Afrikaans and English were officially recognised languages.

South Africa currently has 11 official languages: the most widespread and commonly spoken are Afrikaans and then English, followed by various Bantu languages including Ndebele, Tsonga, Xhosa (the second most frequently spoken Bantu language) and Zulu, which is the predominant Bantu language spoken in the country.

3.6 Style and Language

Afrikaans is a dialect of Dutch. Since the colonisation of southern Africa it has been the most commonly spoken language amongst both whites and native populations in the colonised regions. It began to develop as a distinct dialect in the 18th century. The vocabulary of Afrikaans is 90–95% the same as Dutch: the major differences are in grammar and accent. Afrikaans used to be called "Cape Dutch", to identify its geographical relevance: it was also known as "Kitchen Dutch", which was an insulting term used in the 18th century to distinguish it from the more acceptable "High Dutch". Its current name comes from the Dutch name Afrikaans-Holland, which means African Dutch.

There are lots of **Xhosa words and phrases** used throughout *Mother to Mother*. Mandisa and all of the other black characters in the novel are Xhosa, and while they all speak English and Afrikaans, Xhosa is their tribal language, their mother tongue.

Mother tongue

There is no need for readers to be worried about the use of Xhosa (or Afrikaans) within the text, however, as the words and phrases in these languages **are almost always explained in English**. The context can also usually help in understanding what a word or phrase means.

Archaic and unusual diction

"What, for the homing morrow?" (Mandisa on p. 5) is an example of language use which is very unusual to Western ears. "Homing" makes a verb out of home, meaning to go home – this is about Amy Biehl returning to the USA – which is a very **unusual use of English**. "Homing" as a verb is normally only used in English very specifically,

Language in South Africa

3.6   Style and Language

for example in reference to either homing pigeons (*Brieftauben*) or homing beacons (*Zielflugfunkfeuer*). "Morrow" on the other hand is a **very old-fashioned** and rather literary way of saying tomorrow, and is almost never used in modern English.

This odd vocabulary and the unusual sentence structure are examples of how the various languages spoken by most South Africans – **Afrikaans and English plus at least one Bantu language** – have influenced and subtly changed one another, each of the languages leaving their impressions on the other as the speakers switch back and forth between them throughout their lives.

3.7 Approaches to Interpretation

SUMMARY

Mother to Mother can be read and interpreted as an almost-autobiographical book focussed on real events, and at the same time it can be interpreted on a symbolic level, with Mxolisi and the white girl representing much larger issues than their specific lives and actions.

Mother to Mother is open to a couple of apparently opposed interpretations. On the one hand it is an autobiographically-rooted story concerning real events in real places, and on the other hand, it suggests symbolic meanings which go far beyond the concrete realities of township life.

What unites these differing approaches is the sense of continuity, history and the connectedness of things. Real world events and individuals are never isolated in time and space. They are small parts of a much larger whole. Sindiwe Magona sees her characters as being individual elements in a much larger, ongoing story: the story of the Xhosa tribes, of the colonised and oppressed native peoples of South Africa as a part of the history of the country. **Mandisa and Mxolisi are not isolated characters** acting out their parts on an empty stage, whose thoughts and actions have relevance only to themselves. They are moving parts of a continuously evolving tradition, and as such they are the natural development of what has come before them and are in constant **dialogue with their history** and the history of their people and country. At the end of the novel this idea becomes much clearer.

Embedded in a historical context

This book is not a work of non-fiction and it is not a journalistic account of the killing of Amy Biehl, but it is **inspired by and**

Informative

3.7   Approaches to Interpretation

concerned with real events and their origins and causes. Being as autobiographical as it is, *Mother to Mother* is also rooted in reality and told from the perspective of someone who has lived through and experienced exactly what is being described.

Autobiographical parallels

The author Sindiwe Magona is older than her character Mandisa, but there are parallels in their lives. They lived in the same places, and Magona was also a **single mother** at a young age (although not as young as Mandisa – Magona was 19 when she had her first child). They both live through **apartheid** and into its aftermath – although Magona, being born in 1943, actually lived through the entire apartheid era). Whereas Magona was able to take every opportunity and get herself educated, allowing her to achieve her potential, leave the townships and make a better life for herself, working for the United Nations and becoming a world-famous author, **Mandisa is unable to break away**. Circumstances keep her held down: her three children, poverty, and a deep despair from which she never recovered. Despite the differences, Mandisa's perspective on the world and events around her are informed by the author's own **experiences and observations**. Sindiwe Magona lived through this era.

Differences

Many concrete social issues are addressed in the book and are relevant to the lives of the characters and to the themes Magona addresses. The two most important ones in the novel are the forced resettlements and the issue of education.

→ Mandisa describes her own experiences of the **forced resettlements** from slums like Blouvlei in the Transkei into the newly-built townships like Guguletu, and how this development negatively affected families and entire communities, and concentrated social problems in densely-populated environments.

→ **Education** is a focus for much of the social and political frustrations of the black communities. For the black population

3.7 Approaches to Interpretation

education is so bad, so mismanaged and unjust (teaching biased, incorrect accounts of Xhosa history, rejecting native languages etc.), that from the mid-1970s on there are growing waves of boycotts of the schools, which not only create a violent protest culture and increasingly radicalised generation, but also make sure that millions of young people received no education, let alone a bad one.

Connected to both of these larger issues is the problem of the **violence of the youth movements** (see pp. 73–78). This is the web Mxolisi is caught in: He lacks education (he is 20 years old but still technically in the class for 14-year olds, and he never attends school anyway) and has no way out of a place in which there is no support for him. Guguletu is for Mxolisi and others like him **a kind of open prison**. They wander in large groups around in the streets looking for a place to meet, where they are mobilised by activists. They want to have a better life but don't seem to understand what that could be or how to achieve it. Mandisa is frustrated at **the laziness, disrespect and violence of the younger generations**. She understands that the adults are to blame for having taught the young to be Young Lions, to be angry and to direct their hatred towards the white oppressors. But by 1993, the time of the novel, this violence has got out of hand. In the real world, and in the novel as well, this climaxed in events like **the killing of Amy Biehl**, who was guilty only of being white in the wrong place at the wrong time.

Life in the township

Chapter 5 in the novel contains a personal and detailed description of the **process of forced resettlements** which drove so many tribespeople from their homes into the townships. Mandisa remembers her childhood in Blouvlei: the rumours about the relocations, which no one took seriously, and then the brutal event itself, with **police and military forces** literally destroying the settlements and driving the inhabitants into an uncertain exodus.

Forced resettlement

3.7   Approaches to Interpretation

Abandoned
children

Mandisa makes it very clear throughout the book that the move from Blouvlei to Guguletu was a bad, bad thing, resulting in a **breakdown of communities**, a loss of rights, and **increased levels of depression and crime** throughout the black population. The housing the families are forced into changes them, the breaking up of the old communities has left children with little support, and as more and more mothers and fathers are forced to work badly-paid jobs for long hours far away from their homes, the children are increasingly left to their own devices, growing up without the close attention they would have received in the older communities, such as Gugululu. Poverty and social neglect combine to make the townships dangerous, unhealthy places to live.

Symbolic: nothing happens or exists in a vacuum

The excursions into history, myth and tribal traditions encourage the reader to see the story and the characters in a larger, more symbolic light (see in particular Mandisa's grandfather's lessons, pp. 173–183).

Consequences

Much of Sindiwe Magona's message in the book is that nothing happens or exists in a vacuum. Traditions bring continuity; disruptions cause chaos; events have consequences. Every single person and event is a small part of a much greater whole. This inclusive, all-embracing attitude to the world and to life means that when we read and try to interpret *Mother to Mother*, we must do so in a way that acknowledges **the history of South Africa and the violence the apartheid regime** has done to centuries-old tribal structure and traditions.

Mxolisi: special

The character of Mxolisi can be interpreted as being a symbol of the lost young black men of his country's history. The bizarre circumstances of his conception add to the sense that he is somehow different from those around him; because he is somehow marked as

3.7 Approaches to Interpretation

being different, we as readers can see that the author has identified him as being special. Even before the explicit symbolic statements at the end of the novel, which we will look at below, we have an idea that he represents more than just a little boy in a poor black family. The intense struggles Mandisa has with him are mirrored in her accounts of the history of the violence of the youth movement: She is guilty of having let him down, and **adults are guilty of having let down the younger generations**; she has spoilt her son with love and freedom, and the older generations have allowed the younger generation to run too free and too wild. She also hates and fears her son, as older people hate and fear the wildness and disobedience of the young.

Early in the book there is a juxtaposition of the white girl and Mxolisi: her diligent, optimistic sunny approach to life is contrasted with his laziness and discontent (see pp. 9–10). The intentional comparison of these two opposite individuals becomes even more clearly charged with symbolic meaning at the end of the novel. Mandisa says that Mxolisi and the white girl are the "perfect demon" and "imperfect atonement" of their respective races (p. 201) – this encourages us **to see these figures as symbolic of a larger tragedy**, the crashing together of the authoritarian racism of white colonial powers and the hatred and violence this created within the black indigenous people of the country.

Mxolisi and the white girl: polar opposites

But there is more at the end: There are three sets of paired statements about the dead white girl and Mxolisi in which the two are very explicitly framed as being **symbols of the racism, hatred and conflict** that has defined South Africa's history since the very first appearance of European explorers (see pp. 201–210).

"Your daughter. The imperfect atonement of her race.
My son. The perfect host of the demons of his." (p. 201)

3.7 Approaches to Interpretation

"One boy. Lost. Hopelessly lost.
One girl, far away from home." (p. 210)

"My son, the blind but sharpened arrow of the wrath
of his race.
Your daughter, the sacrifice of hers. Blindly chosen. Flung
towards her sad fate by fortune's cruellest slings." (p. 210)

Mxolisi is explicitly symbolised as weaponised hatred, and the girl as a sacrifice. The huge issue of atonement for **the sins of centuries** is addressed here, but the girl is "imperfect" in this sense – nothing can really atone for three hundred years of brutal racist oppression. As a sacrifice she is random ("blindly chosen"). But Mxolisi is "perfect" as a host for the "demons" (hatred, violence) of his people, a "bind but sharpened arrow", a weapon which was fired centuries ago and finds its target in 1993.

Puppets of history

The symbolism here suggests that these two individuals are **not free and independent characters**, but that they are the agents of

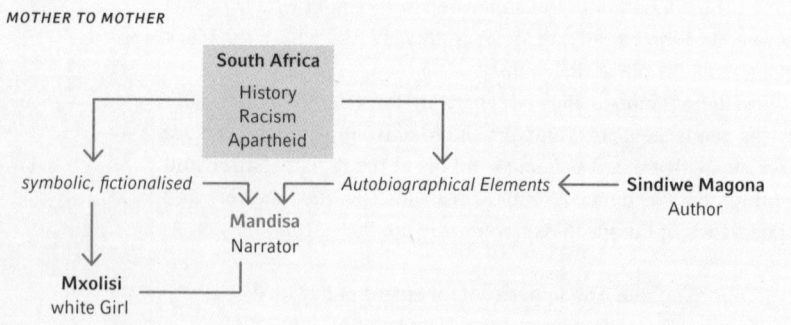

MOTHER TO MOTHER

South Africa
History
Racism
Apartheid

symbolic, fictionalised ← *Autobiographical Elements* ← **Sindiwe Magona** Author

Mandisa
Narrator

Mxolisi
white Girl

3.7 Approaches to Interpretation

forces which have been in motion for hundreds of years. These forces are bigger than any individual: Mxolisi is the creation of his people's history and environment. The girl is a sacrifice.

This symbolic level to the novel is not separate from the concrete concerns with education and social depression. The essential message is that **everything is connected** and everything is informed by what happened before.

4. CRITICAL RECEPTION

SUMMARY

> *Mother to Mother* was universally acclaimed and remains the
> most famous of Magona's works.

The novel was published in 1998, five years after the killing of Amy
Biehl, of which it is a fictionalised account. Twenty years later it is still
widely read and available all around the world. It was successfully
adapted for the stage in 2009 in the form of a monologue (Mandisa
speaking). The critical reaction at the time was overwhelmingly
positive. Here are some examples of reviewers' reactions to the
novel.[16]

> "Magona has succeeded in her grand ambition to write a
> story of healing and confrontation. She has written a graceful,
> terrible story; it is an eloquent indictment of Apartheid and a
> passionate lament over the loss of Amy Biehl's life."
> (Angela Salas *The Boston Book Review*)

> "As a lament for the terrible legacy of apartheid, the novel
> is surely a tour de force. As a story of individuals attempting to
> deal with choices made and perhaps regretted, it is a moving
> work of fiction. (Lee Milazzo *Dallas Morning News*)

> "Gripping. . . . Points to a redemptive hope for those who can
> come together for healing, even when they have been bound
> together by sorrow. The writer's own courage in writing this

16 Reviews taken from: http://sindiwemagona.wixsite.com/website/mother-to-mother

novel is evidence of an increasingly powerful literary voice for [her] nation. (Heather Hewett *The Washington Post Book World*)

What these and other positive reviews make clear is that most people reacted to two features of the novel: the eyewitness account (even if in fiction) of life under apartheid, and the powerful emotional content of the book. As outlined in the chapter in this book on interpretations, it is these two structures which give the book its power: on the one hand, a concrete, informative account of aspects of life under apartheid, making use of real events and places, and on the other hand a narrative with more emotional and symbolic intent which points to the larger human issues beyond the specifics of time and place.

See Chapter 3.7

5. MATERIALS

This chapter contains a brief history of South Africa, a biography of Amy Biehl and some notes on terms which are useful when interpreting and discussing the book.

A brief overview of the history of South Africa

YEAR[17]	EVENT
Ca. 500 BC	The original inhabitants of South Africa, the Han people, begin to form larger organised tribes and start keeping livestock.
Ca. 250 AD	The Bantu peoples from further north in Africa migrate south. They bring with them skills and knowledge in farming and working with metal, as well as new languages.
1488, 1497	The first European explorers, Bartolomeu Dias and Vasco de Gama, sail around the tip of Africa.
1652	The Dutch East India Company establishes a settlement, the Dutch Cape Colony.
1795	The British occupy the Cape, driving out the Dutch after a battle.
1802	The Dutch take back control of the Cape following a peace agreement with the British.
1806, 1814	After another battle, the British take back control of the Cape. In 1814 the Dutch formally acknowledge that the Cape belongs to the British.
1816, 1828	Shaka Zulu forms the Zulu Kingdom, a powerful force in the country. After he is assassinated by his brothers in 1828 the Zulu Kingdom falls apart.

---

17   BCE = Before Christian Era, CE = Christian Era

YEAR	EVENT
1833	An important year: the British forbid the practice of slavery. The descendants of the Dutch settlers, called the Boers, do not agree with this and begin what they call the Great Trek. They head further inland from the Cape and form their own republics, the Orange Free State and the Transvaal, taking land from the tribes living there.
1880	The First Boer War begins between the British and the Boers, who win independence for their two states.
1880s–1890s	Diamonds and gold are discovered in large quantities in South Africa. This leads to a gold rush and the rapid growth of settlements and cities, especially Johannesburg.
1889, 1910	The Second Boer War: The British take the Boers' free states away from them. The Union of South Africa is formed in 1910, as a part of the British Empire, including the former Boer states.
1912	The African National Congress (ANC) is formed. The goal from the beginning was to win voting rights for black and mixed-race Africans. From the 1940s onwards, the primary goal of the ANC was to end apartheid. It remains to this day the largest and most dominant force in South African politics.
1913	The Natives Land Act enforces by law segregation based on race.
1934	South Africa declares independence from Great Britain.
1948	The government officially adopts apartheid as state policy. Laws are passed to classify the population by race.
1961–1962	ANC leader Nelson Mandela forms an armed branch of the ANC to fight against apartheid. In 1962 he is arrested and jailed for 27 years. He becomes a world-famous symbol for the fight against apartheid and injustice.
1976	The Soweto Uprising: A student protest leads to the death of 176 people. This event and the waves of student protests which follow in later years is relevant to *Mother to Mother* when Mandisa reflects on the violent, angry culture which her son Mxolisi belongs to.
1989	President de Klerk begins to dismantle the apartheid laws and end the system.

YEAR	EVENT
1990	Nelson Mandela is released from prison. He is awarded the Nobel Peace Prize in 1993. He dies in 2013.
1993	Amy Biehl is murdered in Guguletu.
1994	Apartheid is officially repealed (ended by law). Black people can vote for the first time.

Amy Biehl

Amy Biehl was born 26th April 1967 in Santa Monica, California. She graduated from Stanford University and went to South Africa to work with anti-apartheid activists. In South Africa she was enrolled at the University of the Western Cape on a scholarship from the prestigious Fulbright scholarship programme. She was killed by protesters in the township of Guguletu on 25th August 1993.

Biehl was a very socially conscious and energetic activist for human rights. Her death was as described in *Mother to Mother*: When she was driving friends and fellow students of her home to the township, her car was surrounded by a mob of black protesters and she was stabbed and stoned to death. Four young men were convicted of having killed her, but in 1998 they were pardoned by the Truth and Reconciliation Commission (TRC). The TRC was established in 1994 to investigate crimes committed during the apartheid era and to provide pardons for people who had been convicted for political reasons. The men who killed Amy Biehl successfully argued to the TRC that the killing had been a political act.

---

18 https://commons.wikimedia.org/wiki/File:Amy_Biehl_Foundation_Trust_Gugulethu_01.jpg

Amy Biehl
Foundation Trust,
Gugulethu[18]

AMY BIEHL
26 APRIL 1967 - 25 AUGUST 1993
KILLED IN AN ACT OF POLITICAL VIOLENCE.
AMY WAS A FULBRIGHT SCHOLAR
AND TIRELESS HUMAN RIGHTS ACTIVIST.

THE AMY BIEHL FOUNDATION, FOUNDED IN 1997
DEVELOP & EMPOWER YOUTH IN SOUTH AFRIC
THROUGH EDUCATIONAL & CULTURAL PROGRAM

Amy Biehl's parents set up a foundation named after their daughter in 1994 to provide help and support for young people in South Africa's townships, continuing the work their daughter had been involved in.[19] Nelson Mandela mentioned her in his speech accepting the Congressional Gold Medal in 1998, praising the young woman for having worked so hard for the cause of justice and equality in South Africa.[20]

Some useful terms

Plot and story

A story is a telling of connected events. Plot refers to the sequence of these events. Confusingly, both of these terms are interchangeable with the term narrative, which can refer to both the story as a whole and the sequence of events within the story.

Frame narrative (or frame story)

This is a literary technique which sets up an introductory story which then contains the main narrative. In the case of *Mother to Mother*, the frame narrative is Mandisa addressing the mother of the dead white girl. This is a frame story which contains the plot – the sequence of events.

Epistolary

This adjective describes a text which is written in the form of letters. This applies to *Mother to Mother* because it is implied that Mandisa is writing to the mother of the dead white girl, rather than talking to her directly. As a literary technique, the epistolary form is often

---

19   https://amyfoundation.co.za/
20   http://www.americanrhetoric.com/speeches/nelsonmandelacongressionalgoldmedalspeech.htm

used to suggest or imply a greater sense of realism than a more usual novelistic approach using an omniscient narrator (an author's voice which appears to know everything about the world and the characters – in contrast to this perspective, an epistolary novel is like a first-person perspective in that it suggests to the reader that what is being narrated is real).

Chronology

Literally the logic of time (from the ancient Greek), this term means the order in which events happen. Typically, the chronology of a narrative is linear – it starts at the beginning and moves through a sequence of events following one another until it reaches "the end". This is obviously not the case in *Mother to Mother*. The chronology of the narrative is non-linear, meaning that it does not start at the beginning of what is being narrated – technically, that would be Mandisa's earliest memories – and progress through to Mandisa being led to Mxolisi's hiding place in August 1993. Instead the chronology of the narrative is very mixed up, and Mandisa (and we the readers) access different points along the timeline. This is done to highlight the origins of events now, and to emphasise themes and ideas which recur through time.

Colonialism and Postcolonial literature

Colonialism is literally the settling and occupation of one culture or nation by another, usually more powerful culture or nation. This is what happened in South Africa with the European – first Dutch, then British – settlers. They didn't just move to South Africa to live there with the original inhabitants of the country, they took over and assumed control. The issue of colonialism in literature and how it should be analysed has become one of the most important fields in literary studies since the mid-20th century, and is known as Postcolonial theory. Before then the overwhelming majority of published literature available in Western countries was produced by colonising cultures rather than the colonized themselves. This began to change after the Second World War. *Mother to Mother* is of course written by a woman who comes from the colonised culture. It is a perfect example of Postcolonial literature: it is concerned with the problems and consequences of a colonized country, in particular themes like race, racism and injustice, and it is written by and from the perspective of one of the colonized people.

6. SAMPLE EXAM QUESTIONS AND ANSWERS

Die Zahl der Sternchen bezeichnet das Anforderungsniveau der jeweiligen Aufgabe.

Task 1: **

In an interview in 2012 with the newspaper *The Scotsman*,[21] Sindiwe Magona talks about how as a girl she had been friends with the mother of one of the boys convicted of murdering Amy Biehl. She says: "I was conscious that although the grief of the bereaved parents is terrible, the grief of the killer's parents is almost worse, because of the terrible questions they must ask themselves – what did I do, or not do, that my child should have become this thing?" Do you agree with this perspective? It is also very much a part of the novel. Do you find it convincing?

Model answer:

This opinion may seem to be controversial at first, but Magona argues convincingly in *Mother to Mother* that the guilt felt by the parents of a killer could be harder to bear than the grief felt by the parents of someone who has been killed. Mandisa says that the other mother feels no shame, because she did everything right. She raised her daughter to be honest and helpful and charitable. She was a friendly and confident young woman who went to another

---

21 https://www.scotsman.com/lifestyle/culture/theatre/interview-sindiwe-magona-writer-and-author-of-mother-to-mother-1-2453210

country to help less fortunate people. The grief she then feels at the death of her daughter could be described as "pure" – unlike Mandisa's grief over her son's actions. Mandisa has to struggle with a lot of guilt and shame: guilt because she worries that she may in some way have been responsible for making him Mxolisi the way he is, and shame because she knows that people around her will blame her for having raised a monster.

The grieving parents of a murdered child can be expected to receive support from those around them, but the parents of a killer can at best hope to be ignored and shunned. More likely, they will spend the rest of their lives being accused of having been responsible for the actions of their child.

These ideas are looked at in *Mother to Mother* when Mandisa directly addresses the other mother. Mandisa at no point suggests that her grief is bigger or worse or more important than the other mother's. She merely tries to explain how the factor of guilt can make her grief more complicated.

Task 2: **

> **Mother to Mother is written in the form of what may be a
> letter to the mother of the white girl who was murdered.
> Why do you think the author chose this particular form for
> her novel?**

Model answer:

Epistolary novel

The story of *Mother to Mother* could have been told in any number of ways, but the form Sindiwe Magona has chosen is unusual because it is so personal.

The style and language is very diverse, and the sections (in italics) in which she directly addresses the other mother ("you") certainly read like a letter someone would write. These sections are scattered amongst other longer sections of text which do not read as if they would be in a letter: Mandisa's lengthy memories of her childhood, for example, are filled with the kind of descriptions and reflective commentaries which we are used to reading in prose fiction. She also writes about these past events as if with no knowledge of the future, reinforcing the distance of fiction. So the novel as a whole cannot really be read as a letter directed to the other mother: Certain sections of it certainly seem to be, but the larger part of it has the style and structure of fiction (however autobiographical it may be).

By making the direct passages in the novel a letter, Magona is placing herself, as author, in the role of the narrator and writer of the letter, and we the readers are in the role of the person receiving the letter – the mother of the dead girl. The narrator is explaining her world and life to us, because we (the American mother) are outsiders who can know nothing about growing up black under apartheid. This is a fitting and appropriate format for a novel which draws so heavily on the author's life and experiences.

Narrator and recipient

The full effect of the novel, with the integration of such an intimate form as a letter within a more conventional literary text, allows the direct and powerful emotional impact of the one mother's voice to be supported and embedded within an effectively rich, descriptive and informative text which gives us as readers a fuller, more artful impression of Mandisa's world than the letter itself would have done. So the novelistic aspects of the book satisfy our needs as readers of fiction, while the letter-like texts within provide a powerful emotional intensity which reinforces the truths of the book, which is rooted in real events and places.

Task 3: ***

Compare and contrast the reactions to Mandisa's pregnancy from those around her.

Model answer:

The people who react most strongly to Mandisa's pregnancy are her mother, her aunt Funiwe, and China, the father of the baby. All three react in very different ways, and the ways in which they react tell us a lot about their characters.

Funiwe

Funiwe is the first to guess that Mandisa is pregnant when she sees her in Gungululu: "[...] twice I found her staring at me [...]. How sharp her eye to have discerned what the experienced one of Makhulu's had failed to see" (p. 109). She is puzzled and confused by Mandisa's claims that she had not had sex with China, but her puzzlement means only that she doesn't understand what has happened, not that she doesn't believe her niece. Once the village wise woman has checked and confirmed that Mandisa is still a virgin, Funiwe is completely on the girl's side: "This child has not disgraced the name of the family", she says (p. 113). She considers the pregnancy to be a "sad accident". She says that the bad opinions of other people shouldn't matter: "What do you care for such small-minded, mean people?" She insists: "We must support and protect her now. How do you think she must be feeling?"

Mandisa's Mama

In stark contrast, Mandisa's mother is furious and ashamed. She comes immediately to Gungululu when she learns what has happened. She reacts with stunned shock and then she cries: "A torrent of tears gushing unchecked down her cheeks" (p. 113). She then starts wailing, "as though announcing the death of a beloved, honoured relative" – instead of responding to the news that her daughter is going to give birth, bringing new life into the world.

The first thing Mandisa's mother says is: "'What will the church people say?' [...] The shame to the family would surely kill her, she said." (p. 113) Despite Makhula and Funiwe trying to persuade her to be kinder to her daughter and to show more love and support, "not once did she indicate that she considered me an innocent victim and therefore someone worthy of her sympathy" (p. 114).

Mandisa's mother's reactions don't soften during the pregnancy. It is only much later when Mandisa and Mxolisi have to go and live with China's family that her mother betrays some sign of affection for the baby.

China's reaction is just as bad. They finally arrange to meet again when Mandisa returns from her exile in the village. "No greeting came. [...] China's face, a mask carved from the hardest wood [...]. Did I have something to fear from China?" (p. 121) His hardness and coldness alarms Mandisa: She was so much looking forward to seeing him again, being completely infatuated with the boy, that she hadn't considered that he wouldn't be just as happy to see her. He had been in love with her as well, writing her love letters while they were separated. When she tells him everything she knows, he at first seems to want to deny it: "I could see he didn't want to hear a thing about his being a father-to-be" (p. 122). And then he accuses her of having been impregnated by someone else: "Mandisa [...]. Go and find whoever did this to you." (p. 122) He then tells her that he has got a scholarship and can go and study at boarding school. Mandisa becomes increasingly angry with him, and sees for the first time "another side to the boy I had so adored [...]. China was vain. Self-centred. And weak. He was a low-down heartless cur." (p. 123)

China

We learn a lot about these characters from their reactions. Funiwe's response is concern followed by unconditional love and support. She is concerned with Mandisa's well-being, as well as with the girl's feelings. She understands that Mandisa is young and un-prepared, scared and confused. Her compassion is a strong sign of the basic goodness within her.

Mandisa's mother reacts with dramatic shock and distress. She cries and howls and wails, and the first thing she appears to be concerned with is the shame she will feel when confronted by her friends and neighbours. She betrays no sign of sympathy with Mandisa or concern for her predicament. Her initial reaction is the same as with Nono, when she becomes pregnant with Mandisa's brother's baby: The mother wouldn't dream of blaming Khaya – she blames the girls in both cases. We learn from her reactions that she is obsessively concerned with appearances and status within the community, even more so than she is with the well-being and happiness of her own daughter. Mandisa's mother is not bad or evil, but she is cold and hard, and has a worrying tendency to dislike and put down other females. She evidently considers girls and women to be more deserving of blame than boys and men.

China – a great disappointment

China's reaction exposes his true nature in a more radical way. Mandisa knows that her aunt is a fun, loving person. She also knows that her mother is strict and obsessive about proprieties. But she had been blinded to China's flaws by her teenage infatuation, and when he reveals himself to be, as she says, vain, self-centred and weak, she is saddened and shocked, but above all angry. She comes to hate him for his weakness and shallowness. In this one moment he reveals more about his character than Mandisa had ever guessed, and her disappointment is complete.

SOURCES & REFERENCES

Edition used for this study guide:
Magona, Sindiwe: *Mother to Mother*. Stuttgart: Ernst Klett
Sprachen, 2016.

About the author:
http://sindiwemagona.wixsite.com/website/biography
https://en.wikipedia.org/wiki/Sindiwe_Magona
Magona, Sindiwe Dr.: *Poverty is not invincible*. TEDx Talks,
7.12.2016. https://www.youtube.com/watch?v=ohgIO0buLb8
Mcmillan, Joyce: Interview: Sindiwe Magona, writer and author of Mother to Mother. In: *The Scotsman*, August 6, 2012.
https://www.scotsman.com/lifestyle/culture/theatre/interview-
sindiwe-magona-writer-and-author-of-mother-to-mother-1-
2453210

Secondary literature on *Mother to Mother*:
Ginkel, Armin: *Lektürehilfe: Mother to Mother*. Independently Pub-
lished, 2017.
Kowalewski, Vera; Proszowski, Lukas: *Begleitheft zur Lektüre
Mother to Mother*. Klett Sprachen: Stuttgart, 2016.

About South Africa:
http://www.sahistory.org.za/
 → This site provides access to a huge archive of documents,
studies, essays, articles and information about virtually every
aspect of South Africa throughout its history. Navigating the
site is not always easy: the layout could be better. But it is an
invaluable resource for anything you may want to find out about
the country. The texts are also all painstakingly sourced and

annotated, giving you information on the primary sources for the essays and articles. One particularly useful feature is the timeline, which allows you to locate texts and information on a specific point in the country's history.

http://www.saha.org.za/imagesofdefinace/copyright.htm
→ Extensive and fascinating online gallery of South African protest posters

Bundeszentrale für politische Bildung: *Das Ende der Apartheid-Gesetze*. 28.1.2016. http://www.bpb.de/politik/hintergrund-aktuell/219628/apartheid-gesetze

Byrnes, Rita M.: *South Africa : a country study*. Federal Research Division, Library of Congress: Washington, D.C., 1997. https://www.loc.gov/resource/frdcstdy.southafricacount00byrn
→ General study of South Africa, including information on education

Guguletu murder rate: *Over 700 murders in Gugulethu since 2005*. 16.11.2010. https://mg.co.za/article/2010-11-16-over-700-murders-in-gugulethu-since-2005

Mandela, Nelson. Speech Accepting the Congressional Gold Medal. delivered 23 September 1998, Washington, D.C. http://www.americanrhetoric.com/speeches/nelsonmandelacongressionalgoldmedalspeech.htm

Matsebula, Jubalane: *Young Lions: The Changing Face of South African Youth Politics 1944–1994*. Edith Cowan University, 1996.
http://ro.ecu.edu.au/cgi/viewcontent.cgi?article=1721&context=theses_hons → The Young Lions: youth violence and student protests

Migration to Cape Town in the Early Twentieth Century.
http://www.capetown.at/heritage/history/1910_dev_immig_art.htm

Seekings, Jeremy: *The 'Lost Generation': South Africa's 'youth problem' in the early -1990s*. In: Transformation 29, 1996. http://pdfproc.lib.msu.edu/?file=/DMC/African%20Journals/pdfs/transformation/tran029/tran029007.pdf → South Africa's "youth problem"

Taylor, Paul: *Young Lion's eager to roar in S. Africa*. In: The Washington Post, April 18, 1993. https://www.washingtonpost.com/archive/politics/1993/04/18/young-lions-eager-to-roar-in-s-africa/bdf3ed25-d83c-46e9-aeeb-e2430645c211/?utm_term=.1daa4a12e006 → More on the Young Lions: this is a very useful article about the youth protest movement written and published just a few months before the murder of Amy Biehl

About Amy Biehl:

Herman, Jan: *Amy Biehl Was a Casualty of the System*. In: *Los Angeles Times*, January 27, 1994. http://articles.latimes.com/1994-01-27/news/ol-16092_1_amy-biehl

Amy Biehl's murderers receive amnesty from TRC. South African History Online, March, 16, 2011. https://www.sahistory.org.za/dated-event/amy-biehl039s-murderers-receive-amnesty-trc

Changing Lives. Former Amy Biehl Foundation. https://amyfoundation.co.za/

Others:

Manser, Martin; Curtis, Stephen: *The Penguin Writer's Manual*. London: Penguin, 2002.

Mbokodoawards 2012: http://www.mbokodoawards.co.za/mbokodo_awards_2012_winnewi.html

https://www.globalsecurity.org/military/world/europe/saracen.htm → Saracens: the armoured vehicles the SA police used in the townships

(All Internet pages last retrieved on 21.5.2018.)

INDEX

apartheid 11, 12, 14, 15, 17–21, 23, 24, 30, 34, 35, 56, 59, 107, 122, 129, 130, 142

autobiographical 6, 8, 29, 36, 119, 120

Biehl, Amy 6, 8, 11, 12, 23, 31–34, 36, 55, 79, 80, 92, 121, 126, 128, 130, 132, 135, 143

Blouvlei 7, 11–13, 37, 40, 44, 63, 65, 78, 80, 99, 106, 120–122

Botha, P. W. 20

cattle killing movement 21, 23, 51, 100, 101, 107

De Klerk, F. W. 20, 129

education 12, 16, 24, 26, 27, 40, 43, 47, 57, 95, 107, 120, 142

Gordimer, Nadine 10

Guguletu/Gugulethu 6, 7, 9, 11–13, 17, 23, 31–33, 35–40, 42, 44, 53, 54, 64–66, 69, 75, 78, 80, 81, 85, 86, 94, 98, 99, 106, 107, 109, 120–122, 130, 142

Gugululu 31, 101, 122

guilt 8, 56, 58, 70, 84, 91, 95, 97, 108–110, 112, 135

identity 8, 59, 71, 84, 85, 89, 100–102, 113

language 8, 25, 114, 117

Mandela, Nelson 20, 34, 129, 130, 132, 142

resettlement 7, 13, 17, 40, 64, 121

United Nations (UN) 9, 18, 21

Xhosa 6–8, 10, 12, 21, 22, 29, 31, 51, 62, 63, 77, 84, 86, 101, 102, 113, 114, 116, 117

Young Lions 26, 92, 94, 121, 142, 143